Richard Pipes is Baird Professor of Hi
Harvard University. He lives in Cambridge, Massachusetts
and New Hampshire.

By Richard Pipes

Russia Under the Old Regime
The Russian Revolution
Russia Under the Bolshevik Regime
Property and Freedom
A Concise History of the Russian Revolution
Communism

Other titles in the Phoenix Press
Universal History Series

The Renaissance *Paul Johnson*
The Balkans *Mark Mazower*
Islam *Karen Armstrong*
The German Empire 1871–1919 *Michael Stürmer*
The Catholic Church *Hans Küng*
Peoples and Empires *Anthony Pagden*
Hitler and the Holocaust *Robert Wistrich*

COMMUNISM
A HISTORY OF THE INTELLECTUAL
AND POLITICAL MOVEMENT

Richard Pipes

PHOENIX

A PHOENIX PAPERBACK

First published in Great Britain in 2001
by Weidenfeld and Nicolson
This paperback edition published in 2002
by Phoenix Press,
an imprint of Orion Books Ltd,
Orion House, 5 Upper St Martin's Lane,
London WC2H 9EA

Second impression 2003

A CIP catalogue record for this book
is available from the British Library

ISBN 1 84212 484 6

Printed and bound in Great Britain by
Clays Ltd, St Ives plc

The most encouraging thing about the Soviet régime was its failure. If it had succeeded ... I would have known that there were no limits to the extent to which human beings could be terrorised and enslaved.

Malcolm Muggeridge[1]

Contents

CONTENTS

Preface

This book is an introduction to Communism and, at the same time, its obituary. For it is quite certain that even if the quest for perfect social equality that had driven utopian communists since antiquity ever resumes, it will not take the form of Marxism-Leninism. The latter's rout has been so complete that even post-Soviet Communists in Russia and elsewhere have abandoned it in favor of an eclectic social democratic platform laced with nationalism. We are, therefore, today able to draw up a balance sheet of a movement that dominated most of the twentieth century, to determine whether its failure was due to human error or to flaws inherent in its very nature.

The word *communism*, coined in Paris in the 1840s, refers to three related but distinct phenomena: an ideal, a program, and a regime set up to realize the ideal.*

* No clear distinction can be drawn between 'socialism' and 'communism.' Marx distinguished two phases of progress toward full communism: first, a transitional phase under which the old inequalities would survive even as their foundations were being destroyed, to be followed by a second, higher phase, in which the principle 'From each according to his ability, to each according to his needs' would replace the principle 'Equal work, equal pay.' Lenin defined the first phase as socialism and the second as communism. However, shortly after seizing power in Russia, he changed the name of his party from 'Social Democratic' to 'Communist,' and we shall use the term Communism to mean Leninist theory and practice. See Andrzej Walicki, *Marxism and the Leap to the Kingdom of Freedom* (Stanford, 1995), 93.

The *ideal* is one of full social equality that in its most extreme form (as in some of Plato's writings) calls for the dissolution of the individual in the community. Inasmuch as social and economic inequalities derive primarily from inequalities of possession, its attainment requires that there be no 'mine' and 'thine' – in other words, no private property. This ideal has an ancient heritage, reappearing time and again in the history of Western thought from the seventh century BC to the present.

The *program* dates back to the middle of the nineteenth century and is most closely associated with the names of Karl Marx and Friedrich Engels. In their *Communist Manifesto* of 1848 Marx and Engels wrote that 'the theory of the Communists may be summed up in a single sentence: Abolition of private property.' Engels claimed that his friend had formulated a scientific theory that demonstrated the inevitable collapse of societies based on class distinctions.

Although throughout history there had been sporadic attempts to realize the communist ideal, the first determined effort to this effect by using the full power of the state occurred in Russia between 1917 and 1991. The founder of this *regime*, Vladimir Lenin, saw a propertyless and egalitarian society emerging from the 'dictatorship of the proletariat' that would eliminate private property and pave the way for Communism.

We shall trace the history of Communism in this sequence both because it makes sense logically and because it is in this manner that it has evolved historically: first the idea, then the plan of realization, and finally the implementation. But we will concentrate on the implementation because the ideal and the program, taken by themselves, are relatively innocuous, whereas every attempt to put them into practice, especially if backed by the full power of the state, has had enormous consequences.

I Communist Theory and Program

The idea of a classless, fully egalitarian society first emerged in classical Greece. Ancient Greece happened to have been the first country in the world to recognize private property in land and to treat land as a commodity, and hence it was the first to confront the social inequalities that result from ownership. Hesiod, a contemporary of Homer (seventh century BC), in the poem *Works and Days* extolled a mythical 'Golden Age' when people were not driven by the 'shameful lust for gain,' when there was an abundance of goods for all to share and mankind lived in perpetual peace. The theme of the Golden Age resounded in the writings of the Roman poets Virgil and Ovid; Ovid spoke of the time when the world knew nothing of 'boundary posts and fences.'

The ideal acquired its earliest theoretical formulation in the writings of Plato. In the *Republic*, speaking through Socrates, Plato saw the root of discord and wars in belongings:

> Such differences commonly originate in a disagreement about the use of the terms 'mine' and 'not mine,' 'his' and 'not his.'...And is not that the best-ordered State in which the greatest number of persons apply the terms 'mine' and 'not mine' in the same way to the same thing?

In *The Laws*, Plato envisioned not only a society in which

people shared all worldly possessions, as well as their wives and children, but one in which

> the private and individual is altogether banished from life, and things which are by nature private, such as eyes and ears and hands, have become common, and in some way see and hear and act in common, and all men express praise and blame and feel joy and sorrow on the same occasions.

Aristotle, Plato's pupil, questioned whether such a communist utopia would bring about social peace, on the grounds that people who hold things in common are more prone to quarrel than those who hold them in private ownership. Furthermore, he argued, the root of social discord lies not in material belongings but in the yearning for them: 'it is not possession but the desires of mankind which require to be equalized.'

There exists a widespread but false notion that socialism and communism are merely up-to-date, secular versions of Christianity. As the nineteenth-century Russian philosopher Vladimir Soloviev has pointed out, the difference is that whereas Jesus urged his followers to give up their own possessions, the socialists and communists want to give away the possessions of others. Moreover, Jesus never insisted on penury; he merely counseled it as easing the way to salvation. Saint Paul's well-known saying about money is usually misquoted: he said not that 'money is the root of all evil' but that '*love* of money' is – in other words, greed. Saint Augustine asked rhetorically, 'Is gold not good?' and answered, 'Yes, it is good. But the evil use good gold for evil, and the good use good gold for good.'

The fathers of the church and later Catholic theologians took a pragmatic view of ownership. According to Saint Augustine, a propertyless world was possible only in paradise – that 'Golden Age' which mankind had lost because of original sin. Given human imperfection, property is moral if used wisely and employed for charitable purposes. The Catholic Church not only did not preach poverty but disowned and sometimes persecuted those who did. The founders of Protestantism, notably Calvin, viewed wealth as a positive good and a sign of divine grace.

But the notion of the Golden Age never disappeared from European consciousness. The early maritime explorers ventured on their journeys inspired not merely by the quest for Eldorado and other mythical places in which gold was reputed to be as plentiful as dust but also by the desire to find the islands of terrestrial paradise, legends of which circulated in medieval Europe. And when they first landed in the Americas and saw naked Indians, they were convinced they had found them: for was not lack of shame the very mark of life before the Fall? If the natives, indeed, lived in paradise this meant also that they knew nothing of property. Columbus on his return reported that the aborigines were 'guileless' and 'never refuse[d] anything which they possess, if it be asked of them; on the contrary, they invite anyone to share it.' He was uncertain whether or not they knew private property, but noted, 'In that which one had, all took a share, especially of eatable things.'

These naive first impressions soon yielded to more realistic appraisals of American Indians, but not before giving rise to a utopian literature that has ever since become a permanent feature of Western thought.* Thomas More's archetypal

* Because the vision of a propertyless society is central to virtually all utopias, it could emerge only in societies in which private property was prevalent: this, until recent times, meant, in effect, Europe and regions populated by Europeans.

Utopia, described in the book of that name he published in 1516, was, some scholars believe, inspired by the travel accounts of Columbus and other early explorers. Far from the happy place that the modern usage of the adjective *utopian* conveys, it was an austere and regimented community where all citizens dressed alike and lived in identical houses, where no one could travel without permission, and where private discussion of public affairs carried the death penalty. Money was abolished; gold and silver served to make chamber pots. The common theme of subsequent utopias was, as in More's, both the absence of private wealth and the coercion of individuals by the community at large: utopia both in theory and practice signifies the individual's subservience to authority, which compels him to do what he is disinclined to do of his own free will.

It needs to be stated at this point that the ideal of a property-less Golden Age is a myth – the fruit of longing rather than memory – because historians, archaeologists, and anthropologists concur that there never was a time or place when all productive assets were collectively owned. All living creatures, from the most primitive to the most advanced, in order to survive must enjoy assured access to food and, to secure such access, claim ownership of territory. During the aeons before humans settled down to pursue agriculture, when they lived primarily by hunting and gathering, kinship groups asserted exclusive access to their area, expelling or killing trespassers. Property claims intensified after transition to agriculture some ten thousand years ago, because cultivation of the soil is arduous work and its fruits take time to mature.

In the oldest civilizations, dating back five thousand years –

pharaonic Egypt and Mesopotamia – agricultural land belonged to palaces and temples. Ancient Israel is the first country where we possess firm evidence of private land ownership. The Lord in the Hebrew Bible casts a curse on anyone who tampers with boundary stones ('Cursed be he that removeth his neighbor's landmark,' Deuteronomy 27:17), and several biblical books tell of families as well as individuals holding land and pasture in private possession. But land ownership in ancient Israel was hedged by many religious and clan restrictions. It is in classical Greece that from the earliest times agricultural land was privately held. In other words, there is no evidence that at any time, even in the most remote past, there existed societies that knew no 'boundary posts and fences' or ignored 'mine' and 'thine.'

A critical contribution to socialist and communist theory was the conception of human nature formulated by thinkers of the Enlightenment. Traditionally, human beings were believed in the West to be made up of body and soul, both given their shape by the Creator; the soul was viewed as filled with ideas and values implanted in it at birth. This was a conservative notion since it posited the immutability of human nature: such as it was, such it would always be. In other words, if man was acquisitive, acquisitive he would remain.

This premise was first challenged by the English philosopher John Locke, who in his *Essay Concerning Human Understanding* (1690) denied the existence of 'innate ideas.' According to him, at birth the mind (or soul) is a clean slate: all ideas and all values derive from sensory experience. This theory implies that human nature is malleable rather than constant and hence that people can be shaped in such a manner that their natural goodness – which the philosophes took for granted – would prevail over selfishness. The French eighteenth-century thinker Claude-Adrien Helvétius made the implicit explicit, arguing that proper instruction and legislation would not only enable but compel humans to attain complete virtue. This highly questionable psychological theory became the common heritage of liberalism, socialism, and communism, which in varying degrees rely on instruction and/or coercion to achieve their respective objectives. In some respects, the Communist state established by Lenin in Russia in November 1917 was a grandiose experiment in public education, undertaken on the Helvétius model for the purpose of creating an entirely new type of human being, one rid of vices, including acquisitiveness.

It was French radical thinkers of the eighteenth century who first advanced communist programs, calling for the abolition of all private wealth on the grounds that it was the cause of every misery known to mankind. In the words of Morelly, the author of the influential treatise *Le Code de la Nature*, published in 1755:

> The only vice which I know in the universe is avarice; all the others, whatever name one gives them, are merely forms, degrees of it...Analyze vanity, conceit, pride, ambition, deceitfulness, hypocrisy, villainy; break down the majority of our sophisticated virtues themselves, [they] all dissolve in this subtle and pernicious element, the *desire to possess*.

Such economically determined psychology lies at the root of every socialist and communist doctrine.

Prior to the middle of the nineteenth century, the ideal of equality was an aspiration that occasionally produced social violence but lacked both a theory and a strategy. Thus, in seventeenth-century England, Gerrard Winstanley, the leader of a radical group called the Diggers, exhorted his followers to seize the commons and turn them into arable land. He formulated something like a communistic doctrine that denounced commerce in land or its product. During the French Revolution, a century and a half later, the French radical François-Noël Babeuf organized a 'Conspiracy for Equality,' which called for the socialization of all property. Neither man, however, had a doctrine capable of demonstrating how the kind of social revolution he advocated would come into being. The same held true of socialist idealists active in the early nineteenth century, such as the Comte de Saint-Simon and Charles Fourier, who pinned their hopes on persuading the rich to part with their wealth.

From time to time there emerged in the West voluntary communist societies. One of them was the Virginia Company in Jamestown (1607); another, New Harmony of Indiana, founded in 1825 by the British philanthropist Robert Owen. All such attempts broke down sooner or later, largely because of their inability to resolve the problem of 'free riders,' members who drew a full share of the community's harvest while doing little if any work.

The contribution of Karl Marx and Friedrich Engels to socialism was a theory that purported to show why the kingdom of equality was not only desirable and feasible but inevitable. To advance this claim, they resorted to methods borrowed from the natural sciences, which had gained immense prestige in the nineteenth century.

7

Marx and Engels formulated a doctrine of 'scientific social-ism,' which asserted that the ideal of a propertyless, egalitarian society was something that not only *should* happen but, by virtue of the natural evolution of the economy, *had to* happen. The Marxist concept of social evolution arose under the influence of the Darwinian theory formulated in 1859 in *On the Origin of Species*. Darwin's book depicted the emergence of biological species as due to a process of natural selection that enabled them better to survive in a hostile environment. The process was a dynamic one, evolving species from lower to higher stages according to determinable rules. This theory was quickly adapted by students of human behavior, giving rise to a school of 'evolutionary sociology' that depicted history as a progression, 'by stages,' from lower to higher forms. So great was Darwin's influence on Marx that Engels, speaking at his friend's funeral, said, 'Just as Darwin had discovered the law of development of organic nature so did Marx discover the law of human history.'

The injection of evolutionary thinking into socialist theory introduced into it the element of inevitability. According to 'scientific socialism,' human actions may somewhat retard or accelerate social evolution, but they cannot alter its direction, which depends on objective factors. Thus, for reasons that will be spelled out below, capitalism in time must inexorably yield to socialism. The emotional appeal of this belief is not much different from the religious faith in the will of God, inspiring those who hold it with an unshakable conviction that no matter how many setbacks their cause may suffer, ultimate victory is assured. It would hold especial attraction for intellectuals by promising to replace spontaneous and messy life with a rational order of which they would be the interpreters and mentors. As Marx put it in a celebrated dictum, 'The philosophers have only interpreted the world in various ways: the point, however, is to change it.' And who is better qualified to 'change' it intelligently than intellectuals?

For all its formal commitment to the scientific method, Marxism violated its most basic feature, namely open-mindedness and a willingness to adjust theory to new evidence. (Bertrand Russell called Bolshevism, an offspring of Marxism, a 'religion' and spoke of its 'habit of militant certainty about objectively doubtful matters.') It was a rigid doctrine, dismissive of different views. Marx made no secret of his attitude toward those who disagreed with him: criticism, he once wrote, 'is not a scalpel but a weapon. Its object is the enemy, [whom] it wishes not to refute but to destroy.' Marxism thus was dogma masquerading as science.

Marxism's adaptation to the scientific culture was only one factor in its appeal. The other had to do with concurrent changes in social conditions. Prior to the Industrial Revolution, the basis of the world's economy had been agriculture. Until then, 80 to 90 percent of Europeans and Americans had lived on and off the land: the rich derived their wealth from the land and the rents it brought. Trade and manufacture, of course, had existed since the remotest antiquity, but they played a marginal role in the economy. Land was the principal source of wealth, for which reason egalitarian movements concentrated on abolishing private ownership of it.

The emergence of large-scale mechanical manufacture changed that. Money from industry and commerce gradually replaced income from rents as the main source of wealth. It also created a new form of poverty, for as mechanization lowered production costs drastically, traditional forms of small-scale, manual production became obsolete and many artisans were thrown out of work.

Industrialization not only caused painful social dislocations but fundamentally and permanently altered relations between employers and employees. Landlords and their tenants had been neighbors and in some respects partners. Although on occasion tenants suffered mass expulsions, as during the Enclosure Acts in England, by and large the countryside was stable, especially in such countries as the United States, where the great majority of farmers owned the soil they cultivated.

In industrial societies, the relationship of owner to employee turned tenuous and volatile, as the former felt free to dismiss workers whenever demand grew slack. Differences in lifestyle became more glaring as the nouveaux riches flaunted their wealth.

These developments led to a growing hostility to 'capitalism.' Socialism, until then an ideal with particular appeal to intellectuals, now acquired, in addition to a theoretical foundation, a social base among certain segments of the working class.

The collected writings of Marx and Engels fill dozens of volumes; *Das Kapital* alone covers some fourteen hundred pages of dense, technical prose. Few people have ever plowed through this difficult literature, and hence one may wonder how to explain its immense influence. The answer is that the basic tenets of the doctrines of 'scientific socialism' can be reduced to several rather simple propositions.

In his address at Marx's funeral Engels described 'the law of human history' his friend is said to have discovered:

that mankind must first of all eat, drink, have a shelter and clothing, before it can pursue politics, science, art, religion etc; that therefore the production of the immediate material means of subsistence...form[s] the foundation upon which the state institutions, the legal conceptions, art, and even ideas on religion of the people concerned have evolved, and in the light of which they must, therefore, be explained, instead of *vice versa*, as had hitherto been the case.

In short, economics is the foundation of organized life: all else is 'superstructure.'

From this premise, Marx and Engels proceeded to formulate a theory of social evolution, the central postulate of which holds that control of the means of production leads to the emergence of social 'classes.' Originally, there was no private property in these means: all land was held in common. But in time, the 'primitive communal' order gave way to class differentiation as one group succeeded in monopolizing the vital resources and used its economic power to exploit and dominate the rest of the population by erecting political and legal institutions protecting its class interests. It also employed culture – religion, ethics, the arts and literature – to the same end. Such devices have enabled the ruling class to exploit the rest of the population.

Of course, the lower classes do not acquiesce peaceably to their exploitation; they resist, although for as long as there is private property they merely succeed in replacing one form of exploitation with another. For this reason, in the words of the *Communist Manifesto*, so far all the history of societies has been the history of class struggles.

Such reflections on the past served Marx merely as a prelude to his main interest, the analysis of the contemporary 'capitalist' world. He spent many years poring over the evidence on English economic history in order to demonstrate that 'capitalism' was the final stage of class society and that it was bound to collapse as the result of a revolution of exploited industrial labor. That revolution would be the last, for it would inaugurate the reign of a classless society. At this point, history would come to a full stop.

The capitalist system rests on the exploitation of wage labor in that the capitalist appropriates the 'surplus value' of what the worker produces. According to Engels, the notion of 'surplus value' was the second great idea that Marx had contributed to human understanding. All value derives from labor. Under the capitalist system, however, the employer pays his workers only a fraction of the value they create – just enough to keep them alive. The excess, or 'surplus,' he pockets.

In the evolution of the capitalist mode of production, both the rate of profit obtained by the capitalist and the wages of the worker steadily decline. This happens because, confronting fierce competition, the capitalist has to spend ever more of his capital on equipment, raw materials, and the like and ever less on wages, which are the source of his profits. Labor becomes cheaper and wages decline, leading to a steady drop in living standards. At the same time, in the course of crises that occur periodically because of overproduction, large enterprises swallow up smaller ones and industrial wealth is concentrated in fewer and fewer hands. Thus the capitalist and the worker find themselves in the same boat, as it were: the former afflicted by crises and expropriation by those richer than he, the latter the victim of progressive 'pauperization.' In time, the situation inexorably leads to revolution:

> Along with the constantly diminishing number of the magnates of capital…grows the mass of misery, oppression, slavery, degradation, exploitation; but with this, too, grows the revolt of the working class, a class ever increasing in numbers and disciplined, united, organized by the very mechanism of capitalist production itself. The monopoly of capital becomes a fetter upon the mode of production…Centralization of the means of production and socialization of labor at last reach a point where they become incompatible with their capitalist integument [enveloping layer]. Thus [the] integument is burst asunder. The knell of capitalist private property sounds. The expropriators are expropriated.[1]

Reforms of the capitalist system cannot prevent this outcome: it is inevitable.

The ultimate result of the socialist revolution will be the total liberation of man. By 'freedom' Marx and Engels did not mean the liberal notion of civil rights and protection from the state: 'Political liberty is sham-liberty,' Engels wrote, 'the worst possible slavery; the appearance of liberty and therefore the reality of servitude.'[2] Along with Engels, Marx rejected liberal freedoms and civil rights as fraud because they enslaved man to material things; genuine liberty will free human beings from subjection to them. What they had in mind is explained by the Marxian theorist George Lukacs:

> The 'freedom' of the men who are alive now is the freedom of the individuals isolated by the fact of property which both

reifies and is itself reified. It is a freedom *vis-à-vis* the other (no less isolated) individuals. A freedom of the egoist, of the man who cuts himself off from others.³*

For this reason, the abolition of property is a prerequisite to genuine freedom. Only after mankind has been liberated from this dependency will it attain complete self-fulfillment. Division of labor, the bane of humanity, will be abolished, and people will be free at will to shift from one occupation to another. Marx mused:

> In communist society, where nobody has one exclusive sphere of activity...society regulates the general production and thus makes it possible for me to do one thing to-day and another to-morrow, to hunt in the morning, fish in the afternoon, rear cattle in the evening, criticize after dinner, just as I have in mind, without ever becoming hunter, fisherman, shepherd or critic.⁴

The theories formulated by Marx and Engels provided the program of the International Workingmen's Association, popularly known as the First International, which they founded in London in 1864 to prepare labor for the approaching crisis of capitalism. The organization was from the first riven by disputes between socialists and anarchists. Although the anarchists shared with the socialists a common goal – a classless

---

* To 'reify' means to assign reality to an abstraction. Marx, following Ludwig Feuerbach, gave as an example the tendency of humans to project all that they regarded as good and desirable onto a non-existent being (in Marx's opinion) that they designated 'God.' Another example is the statement 'History will judge' rather than Historians will judge.'

and stateless society – as well as the means to the end – violent revolution – in three important respects they parted ways with them. The anarchists saw the revolutionary potential not in the industrial working class but in the landless peasantry and the unemployed. Secondly, the socialists envisaged between collapsing capitalism and triumphant communism a transitional stage (sometimes called 'dictatorship of the proletariat'), during which the new ruling class would use the coercive powers of the state to dispossess the bourgeoisie of its capital and nationalize productive assets. The anarchists rejected the state in all its forms, predicting that the 'proletarian dictatorship' would turn into a new instrument of oppression, this time run by and for the benefit of intellectuals. Finally, while the Marxists relied on the natural progression of the capitalist economy to bring about a revolution, the anarchists called for 'direct action,' that is, an immediate assault on the existing system.

Time proved the anarchists right on all three points: social revolutions broke out not in industrial countries but in agrarian ones, and the 'dictatorship of the proletariat' did turn the communist state into a permanent dictatorship of nonworkers over manual laborers and peasants. The Bolshevik revolution in 1917 Russia also was the result of a direct assault on government in a country where capitalism was still in its early phase of development.

Thus, virtually every one of Marx's predictions turned out to be wrong, as became increasingly apparent during his lifetime and incontrovertibly so after his death.

While capitalism did, indeed, experience periodic crises, it never suffered a fatal crisis ending in social breakdown. Due

partly to antitrust legislation, partly to the advances of technology, which opened ever new opportunities for small entrepreneurs, and partly to the steady growth of the service
sector at the expense of manufacture, the consolidation of
businesses did not progress to the point where all that
remained were giant monopolies. The creation of joint-stock
companies helped diffuse wealth.

Nor did labor suffer pauperization. Even while Marx was
working on *Das Kapital* evidence emerged that wages of labor
in England were rising – evidence Marx chose to ignore. More
important still was the introduction of state-sponsored welfare
schemes. The industrial democracies, alarmed by socialist
strides in organizing labor and gaining seats in parliamentary
elections, instituted social legislation in the form of unemployment and health insurance and other benefits that kept the
working class from sinking into destitution. The first country
to take this route was Germany, where the Social Democratic
Party was especially strong and seemed poised to gain a parliamentary majority. As other continental countries followed
suit, workers acquired a stake in the status quo, turning a deaf
ear to socialist calls for revolution: their behavior contradicted
the assertion of the *Communist Manifesto* that 'working men
have no country.' They had ceased to be a 'proletariat' in the
original sense of the word, that is, a class whose only service to
the state consisted of breeding children (*proles*). Accordingly,
they preferred trade-union activity, which accepted the capitalist order and concentrated on obtaining a greater share of capitalism's profits. They thus became a part of the very system
the Marxists wanted them to overthrow.

For all these reasons, no explosion happened in any of the

advanced capitalist countries: such revolutions as did take place in the century following Marx's death occurred, as the anarchists had predicted, in so-called Third World countries with embryonic capitalist economies, large landless or land-poor peasantries, and lawless regimes.

The flaws in the Marxist doctrine would not have mattered much had it been a strictly theoretical construct. But since it was a program of action as well, once its predictions proved false – and this became evident shortly after Marx's death in 1883 – first the socialists and then the communists, even while claiming orthodoxy, began to revise Marx's theory. In the Western democracies these revisions generally softened Marx's revolutionary zeal and moved socialism closer to liberalism. The result was social democracy. In eastern Europe and countries of the Third World, by contrast, the revisions tended to exacerbate the elements of violence. The result was Communism. Marxism in its pure, unadulterated form was nowhere adopted as a political platform because it flew in the face of reality.

The First International broke up in 1876 but revived in 1889, after Marx's death. Known as the Second International, it united socialist parties of various countries (minus the anarchists, whom it excluded), but its mainstay was the German Social Democratic Party. Revolutionary in slogans, evolutionary in practice, the Second International dominated socialist politics until the outbreak of the First World War. Its official platform, the so-called Erfurt Program, adopted in 1891, contended that the interests of the 'bourgeois' state and the working class were irreconcilable and that, accordingly, workers had no stake in their nation: they owed loyalty only to their class. It reaffirmed the international unity of labor and the imminence of a revolution that would crush capitalism and the bourgeoisie around the globe.

Not all socialists accepted this radical doctrine. In all countries of Europe some insisted that, realistically speaking, the progress of the working class would more likely come from political and economic reform rather than violent revolution. The French socialist Jean Jaurès predicted:

> The proletariat will come to power not through an unanticipated blow of political agitation, but by the methodical and legal organization of its own powers under democratic conditions and the universal right to vote. Our society will gradually develop towards Communism, not through the collapse of the capitalist bourgeoisie but by a gradual and inexorable strengthening of the proletariat.

The leading advocate of this course was the English Fabian Society, which counted among its members such literary luminaries as George Bernard Shaw and H. G. Wells. Its program called for 'persuading' the country to emancipate itself from capitalism by nationalizing industry; like the pre-Marxist socialists, the Fabians appealed to the nation's conscience.

The most audacious assault on the premises and agenda of Marxism was undertaken by Eduard Bernstein, a leading light of German social democracy and the founder of socialist 'Revisionism.' Bernstein had spent many years in England, where he came in contact with the Fabians. In the late 1890s he appealed to Social Democrats to adjust their theory as well as their program to the fact that capitalism was not about to

collapse and labor was not sinking into destitution. He continued to believe in socialism but, like Jaurès, thought it would
come about as the result of peaceful political and social
progress within capitalism. He foresaw something like a con-
vergence of capitalism and socialism, with the latter emerging
from the former.

The German Social Democratic Party, Europe's largest and
most influential, rejected Bernstein's Revisionist theories and
continued to adhere to the revolutionary Erfurt Program. In
practice, however, it did exactly what Bernstein advocated,
that is, emphasize trade unionism and electoral politics. (It
formally abandoned Marxism only in 1959.)

Thus European socialism during its heyday, the quarter
century preceding the outbreak of World War I, moved in fact, if
not always in theory, away from violent revolution and toward
peaceful reform. But it steadfastly adhered to the belief in labor's
transnational solidarity. The Second International clung to the
belief that workers of all countries were brothers and that they
had the supreme responsibility to prevent wars unleashed by
capitalism. The subject often came up for discussion at congresses of the International. Various proposals were advanced on
how to prevent war and what to do in case it nevertheless broke
out. The resolution adopted at the Stuttgart congress of 1907 (in
the drafting of which participated two leading Russian Marxists,
Vladimir Lenin and L. Martov) pledged, in case of war, 'to rouse
the masses and thereby hasten the downfall of capitalist class
rule' – in other words, to transform a war between nations into a
civil war between classes. At the next congress, held in 1910,
the delegates unanimously approved a resolution that called on
socialist parliamentarians to vote against war credits.

Unfortunately for them, the socialists and their International proved utterly powerless to prevent the general European war that erupted in the summer of 1914. Talk of a general strike led nowhere. To make matters worse still, both German Social Democrats and French Socialists, contrary to their solemn pledges, voted for war credits, thereby completely discrediting the notion of international worker solidarity. National loyalties overcame class loyalties, a fact not lost on ambitious demagogues like Benito Mussolini and Adolf Hitler, who would rise to power after the war on platforms that fused socialism and nationalism.

The failure of the Second International to make good its antiwar vows dealt a devastating blow to its fortunes. Socialist parties survived the war, but they became increasingly identified with their own nations.

The cause of socialist internationalism now shifted outside western Europe, first to Russia and then to other non-Western countries.

II   *Leninism*

Ever since 1709, when Peter the Great defeated the Swedes at Poltava and ended their hegemony in the Baltic region, Russia was considered and considered herself a Great Power; and as such, she claimed a place in the European community.

This claim was justified, but only up to a point. Saint Petersburg, her capital city, modeled on Amsterdam, was indeed a Western metropolis, and Russia's French-speaking elite felt at home in the West. The emergence in Russia during the nineteenth and early twentieth centuries of a literature, music, art, and science that fitted into contemporary European culture, and in some respects even stood in its vanguard, reinforced this impression.

But high culture represented only a thin layer of Russian society, made up of the nobility, intelligentsia, and upper bureaucracy. Fully three-quarters of the empire's population consisted of peasants who, in the case of the Russian majority, lived in a world of their own, untouched by Western civilization. They had no common language with the educated, whom they viewed as foreigners. Most Russian peasants were not farmers tilling their own soil; rather, they belonged to rural communes that owned the land collectively and periodically redistributed it to adjust each household's holdings to changes in its size. Land, in the peasants' eyes, was not a commodity but a source of livelihood to which only those who tilled it had a rightful claim.

The peasants were conservative, loyal to the monarchy and the Orthodox Church. In one respect, and one only, did they furnish potential raw material for revolution; namely, that they suffered from a land shortage. Russia's peasants were not an oppressed rural proletariat: in 1916, on the eve of the revolution, they owned 89.1 percent of the land under crops in European Russia.[1] But their numbers grew more rapidly than the soil at their disposal: a parcel that in the mid–nineteenth century had fed two mouths fifty years later had to feed three. Their traditional methods of extensive agriculture, aggravated by a difficult climate, produced low yields. They firmly believed that the tsar, whom they regarded as the rightful master of all the land, would any day take it away from the private owners – landlords and fellow peasants alike – and allocate it to the communes. But if he failed to do so – and by the early 1900s they began to suspect that he would – they were prepared to seize it by force. Other factors in her past also contributed to make Russia non-Western. Through much of her history she was ruled by an extreme form of autocracy, under which the tsar not only enjoyed unlimited legislative, judiciary, and executive powers but literally owned the country, in that he could, at will, exploit its human and material resources – the type of regime that the German sociologist Max Weber labeled 'patrimonial.' The administration of the vast empire was entrusted to a bureaucracy that, along with the armed forces and police, maintained order without being accountable to the people. Until 1905, when civil disorders compelled the tsar to grant his subjects a constitution and civil rights,

Russians could be arrested and exiled without trial for merely contemplating changes in the status quo.

Private property in land came to Russia – exclusively to its nobility – only at the close of the eighteenth century; until then, all the land had belonged to the Crown. By contrast, in the West the bulk of the land had been in private hands since the Middle Ages. Legal institutions, which usually develop hand in hand with property rights, also came late: the first law codes appeared in the 1830s and the first effective courts in the 1860s. Until then, the vast majority of Russians, serfs of the state or of the nobles, had neither legal nor property rights. The earliest representative institutions, limiting the power of the Crown, emerged in 1906, centuries after European parliaments had come into being. There was no social legislation. This historical legacy meant that the majority of Russians and the nations they had conquered felt no stake in their government. They obeyed because they had no choice; their ideal, however, was anarchy.

While maintaining a tight grip on the country, the tsars, eager to maintain the status of a great world power, took steps that inadvertently subverted their authority. One was promotion of higher education. By advancing knowledge and critical thinking, Russian universities created a body of citizens who found intolerable the prevailing repressions on speech. Alexander Herzen, a Russian radical of the mid–nineteenth century, thus articulated the dilemma confronting his generation:

> They give us a comprehensive education, they inculcate in us desires, the strivings, the sufferings of the contemporary world, and then they cry: 'Stay slaves, dumb and passive, or else you perish.'

Such inconsistent policies gave rise to the intelligentsia, whose defining quality was opposition to the entire existing political and social order and the conviction that in so doing it was speaking for the mute people. The recruiting grounds for revolutionaries, ranging from nonviolent 'propagandists' to the most extreme terrorists, were not Russia's factories or villages but her universities.

The tsars' other measure that subverted their own authority was the encouragement of capitalism. In the Crimean War of 1854-55, Russia suffered defeat on her own soil at the hands of Western industrial democracies. This humiliation demonstrated that in the modern world no country could lay claim to being a great power unless it acquired significant industry and transport. It persuaded tsars actively to promote their growth with the help of domestic and foreign capital. The result was the emergence of centers of decision making independent of the government and its bureaucracy.

In sum, the advance of education and industrialization required to meet Russia's global ambitions weakened tsarism's hold on the country.

Such factors help explain why the Communist revolution that, according to Marx, was bound to break out in the industrialized West in fact broke out in the agrarian East. Russia lacked the deterrents to social revolution present in the West: respect for law and property, along with a sense of allegiance to a state that protected liberty and provided social services. The Russian radical intelligentsia, permeated with utopian idealism, on the one hand, and a peasantry bent on seizing private land, on the other, created a state of permanent tension liable to explode any time the central government found itself in trouble. None of the economic imperatives posited by Marx and Engels played any role here.

The factors that made Russia prone to erupt in revolution also determined the shape of its Communist regime. As it turned out, socialism introduced into a country lacking the traditions that would make for the ideally self-fulfilling life that Marx had envisioned in no time and quite spontaneously assumed the worst features of the defunct tsarist regime. Socialist slogans, which in the West would be steadily watered down until they became indistinguishable from liberal ones, in Russia and other non-Western countries were reinterpreted in accustomed terms to mean the unlimited power of the state over citizens and their assets. Soviet totalitarianism thus grew out of Marxist seeds planted on the soil of tsarist patrimonialism.

The revolutionary movement in Russia was born in the 1870s under the influence of Western socialist and anarchist doctrines, which gained a following mainly among university students. The youths went to the countryside expecting a warm welcome from the peasants but they met with disappointment. The peasants, it turned out, rather than resenting their richer neighbors, or 'kulaks,' dreamed of becoming kulaks themselves. They believed in the tsar, convinced that he would distribute to them all the land in private possession.

Disillusioned, most radical youths left the movement. But a small core formed into the 'People's Will' Party, committed to breaking down the awe in which the common people held the tsar, to which end it initiated a campaign of assassinations against government officials. The People's Will organized the earliest political terror campaign in history. In March 1881, it succeeded in assassinating Alexander II, the monarch who twenty years earlier had liberated Russia's serfs. The murder failed in its purpose. Indeed, it had the opposite effect: instead of arousing the people against the regime, it generated widespread public revulsion, discrediting, for a time, revolutionary methods.

Social democracy came to Russia in the 1890s. It owed its attraction to the fact that during this decade Russia was undergoing such rapid industrialization that it appeared certain soon to acquire a full-scale capitalist economy with all the attendant social consequences, as outlined in *Das Kapital*. The study groups of Russian social democratic youths that sprouted at the universities at this time rejected terrorism as a futile tactic that sought to anticipate the evolution of the economy. In time, their members believed, Russia would experience all the contradictions inherent in capitalism and erupt in revolution.

The Russian Social-Democratic Labor Party was founded at a clandestine meeting – quickly broken up by the police – held in 1898. Its manifesto, written by Peter Struve, declared that Russia would gain liberty by the efforts not of the timid bourgeoisie but of industrial labor. Liberation from autocracy, in turn, would pave the ground for socialism. This premise hinted at what would become the central postulate of Russian social democracy: the notion of a two-stage revolution, the first to destroy tsarist autocracy and give Russia a democratic 'bourgeois' regime, the next to overthrow this regime and proceed toward socialism. This strategy replicated that advocated by Marx and Engels, which called for a tactical alliance with the liberals against feudal regimes.

The Russian Social-Democratic Labor Party was formally organized in 1903 at a congress held in London. There the movement promptly split into two factions, one headed by Martov and dubbed 'Menshevik,' the other by Lenin, which called itself 'Bolshevik.' Despite attempts at reconciliation, the two factions never reunited, because of Lenin's uncompromising hostility to all socialists who resisted his leadership. Since the term *Communism* came to be largely associated with Lenin and his party, it is necessary at this point to pause and take a closer look at this man, who arguably had a greater impact on twentieth-century politics than any other public figure.

Lenin was born Vladimir Ilich Ulianov in 1870 in the family of a conservative and devoutly Orthodox school inspector in the city of Simbirsk on the Volga. His father's high rank in the official hierarchy qualified him and his offspring for membership in the hereditary nobility. It was not uncommon in late Imperial Russia for the children of such high functionaries, apparently from a sense of guilt over their privileges, to turn radical. In 1887, Lenin's elder brother, Alexander, was executed for involvement in a plot to assassinate Tsar Alexander III. Lenin's sisters also got into trouble and spent time in prison. Lenin himself, however, during his school years showed no interest in politics: an outstanding student, he advanced from class to class, rewarded with gold medals for his studies and exemplary behavior.

His troubles began in 1887, after he had enrolled at the University of Kazan. Here, participation in a minor student disturbance directed against university regulations brought him to the attention of the police. Identified as the brother of an executed terrorist, he was expelled from the university and, despite his widowed mother's repeated requests, denied read-mission. Lenin spent the three years following his expulsion in forced idleness, growing increasingly embittered at a regime that had punished him so severely for a minor infraction of university rules, ruining forever his career. His resentment focused not only on tsarism but also on the 'bourgeoisie' that ostracized his family for the crime of his executed brother. It made him into a fanatical revolutionary determined to destroy, root and branch, the existing social and political order. The source of Lenin's revolutionary passion was thus not sympathy for the poor; indeed, when famine struck the Volga region in 1891–92, he alone among the local intelligentsia opposed humanitarian assistance to the starving peasants, on the grounds that the famine was progressive because it destroyed the old peasant economy and paved the way for socialism. Nor was his revolutionary ardor inspired by a vision of a more just future. It was grounded in anger and driven by a craving for revenge. Struve, who collaborated with him in the 1890s, wrote many years later that the principal feature of Lenin's personal-ity was hatred. And this predisposition of a provincial Russian youth would exert immense influence on twentieth-century politics, the main impulse of which would derive from resent-ment and animosity toward outsiders, whether of a different social class or ethnic and racial group.

In 1891 the authorities finally relented and allowed Lenin to take external examinations for a law degree, which he readily passed, following which he moved to Saint Petersburg. Here he engaged in perfunctory legal practice as a cover for revolution-ary activity. Local social democrats found the newcomer to be less of a Marxist than a disciple of the People's Will, supportive of terror and burning with impatience to launch a revolution without waiting for capitalism to mature. Contacts with the theoretically better-versed socialists converted him – for a while, at any rate – to the idea of a two-stage revolution. Disciplined, energetic, wholly dedicated to the socialist cause, he quickly rose to prominence in the clandestine social democratic movement.

Lenin was arrested in 1896 for encouraging workers to strike and exiled to Siberia. There he lived for three years in relative comfort in a rented cottage with his new bride, Nadezhda Krupskaya, corresponding with friends, writing, and translating. It was during his term of exile (1897–1900) that the Revisionist movement spread in Germany and from there to Russia. Its antirevolutionary program appalled Lenin: it spelled a betrayal of the cause that had attracted him to socialism. He was further distressed by evidence that Russia's nascent labor movement, with which he had only slight personal acquaintance, seemed more concerned with peaceful trade-union activity than with toppling capitalism. These developments precipitated in him a profound spiritual crisis. He emerged from it persuaded that if he could not sway the Social Democrats to adhere to the revolutionary strategy, he would break with the movement and form his own party.

As soon as he had been released from exile, Lenin moved to Germany, where in partnership with Martov he founded the journal *Iskra* (The Spark) to champion the cause of orthodox, anti-Revisionist Marxism. Yet his own views of Marxism were no less unorthodox. In 1902 he published *What Is to Be Done?*, in which he formulated the basic doctrine of what would become Bolshevism. He implicitly rejected the thesis, central to Marxism, that in the course of time the working class was bound to revolt: left to itself, he argued, it was incapable of moving beyond trade unionism. Revolutionary zeal had to be brought to it from the outside by a party of tightly organized professional revolutionaries. Although Lenin did not draw this inference, these people, of necessity, had to be intellectuals, since workers had neither the time nor the theoretical equipment for such a mission.* Indeed, only one solitary worker ever sat on the executive board of Lenin's party, and he turned out to be a police spy.

Lenin came to the 1903 Social Democratic congress fully prepared to split the party and to separate his adherents from the conciliatory majority. The formal reason for the breach was Lenin's insistence that to become a member of the party one had not only to support its program but to commit oneself to full-time revolutionary activity. The party, organized on the military model with a strict chain of command, was to direct labor rather than be directed by it. Having secured a temporary plurality at the congress, Lenin appropriated for his faction the name 'Bolshevik,' i.e., 'majority,' while his opponents, led by Martov, had to be satisfied with the label 'Menshevik,' meaning 'minority.'

The next ten years in the history of the Russian Social-Democratic Labor Party were filled with intrigues and squabbles. Lenin called his Menshevik rivals 'renegades,' 'liquidators,' and other abusive names. To establish a party of professional revolutionaries he needed money, and this he

* Benito Mussolini, the founder in 1919 of the Fascist Party but before World War I leader of the extreme radical wing of Italian social democracy, held at the time similar views.

secured by various unsavory means, including bank holdups and embezzlement of legacies.

During the prewar years, Lenin developed two additional theories. One held that Russia did not have to undergo a 'bourgeois' revolution since she was already in the throes of capitalism and hence ready for a socialist revolution. The second maintained that in striving to overthrow the status quo, the socialists had to enter into temporary alliances with every group that, for its own reasons, also opposed it, in particular the peasantry and the national minorities.

To Marxists, the peasantry was a 'petit bourgeois' class and as such an enemy of industrial labor. Lenin, however, aware of the peasants' desire to get hold of private land, was quite willing to help unleash a rural revolution, confident that after he had seized power he could bring the peasantry to heel by nationalizing the soil. As for the nationalities, like the other socialists he despised nationalism in all its manifestations. But he believed that the nationalist aspirations of the Poles, Finns, and other ethnic groups ruled by Russia could also help undermine the regime. On these grounds he promised every ethnic group the right to self-determination, including the right to separate itself and form a sovereign state. When queried by his followers why he wanted to 'Balkanize' Russia, he would reply that the economic bonds holding the Russian Empire together were too strong to permit separatism, and that even if one or more of the borderlands succeeded in separating themselves they could always be forcibly brought back into the fold on the grounds that 'proletarian self-determination' overrode 'national self-determination.'

Lenin spent virtually the entire period from 1900 to 1917

abroad. In Germany, Austria, Italy, and Switzerland, he worked to split the Second International as he had split the Russian Social-Democratic Labor Party, but he had little success. He maintained contact with his followers in Russia and spent much time writing vitriolic attacks on his opponents. Except for his closest disciples – whom, when they erred, he sought to persuade – anyone else who disagreed with his policy he depicted as a traitor to the working class.

He visited Russia only once during this long period, during the 1905 revolution. The Bolsheviks benefited from the political rights that tsarism had granted in its aftermath to organize in the open. Neither social democratic faction acquired a mass following: in 1907, their combined membership rose to 84,000; in time, as the revolutionary fervor ebbed, the membership melted away, and in 1910 it stood at 10,000 or fewer in a country of over 150 million inhabitants. The Bolsheviks attracted largely Great Russians, while the Mensheviks had a higher proportion of the minorities (such as Jews and Georgians). Neither recruited many workers, being composed overwhelmingly of intellectuals.

Then came the Great War. The Russian social democrats, Mensheviks and Bolsheviks alike, were – with the exception of the Serbians – the only socialists to vote against war credits. For their opposition, the Bolshevik deputies in parliament were arrested and exiled. Their party network was for all practical purposes destroyed.

When the war broke out, Lenin adopted at once an uncompromising position: the war between nations had to be turned into a war between classes. Instead of shooting at one another, the workers should turn their guns against their exploiters.

This position found some adherents in the Second International; they met in neutral Switzerland. The Russians were strongly represented at these conferences, where Lenin assumed leadership of the radical left. His resolutions were not adopted, but even so he exerted strong influence on the proceedings, which laid the foundations of what in 1919 would become the Third, or Communist, International.

Russia entered World War I as an ally of France and Britain. She joined the alliance out of fear that Germany and Austria, in their expansion eastward and southward, would annex her territories and reduce her to the status of a second-rate power. France entered into a military partnership with Russia out of fear of an overpowering German attack, which she could stave off only if Germany had to fight on two fronts. The Russo-French accord called for Russia to attack Germany and promptly to advance on Berlin after the expected German invasion of France.

As things turned out, all the prewar plans of the belligerents went awry. The German Schlieffen Plan, which envisioned a quick and decisive victory on the western front, followed by a transfer of forces to the east to dispose of the Russians, miscarried: the campaign in the west turned into static trench warfare with no resolution in sight. The Russians advanced boldly into East Prussia, only to be trapped and crushed by the Germans.

In late 1914, the German High Command concluded that the only way the war could be won was if Russia were knocked out and Germany could concentrate all her forces on the western front. In the spring of the following year, a joint Austro-German force invaded Russian Poland and drove the tsar's armies hundreds of miles eastward. While the bulk of the Russian forces survived intact and Russia stayed in the war, at least nominally, she lost some of her richest and most populous regions.

These defeats generated in Russia a great deal of discontent, especially in liberal and conservative circles. The liberals in parliament (Duma) demanded that the government concede to it the power to appoint ministers. The conservatives wanted Tsar Nicholas II to abdicate in favor of a more forceful member of the imperial family. Rumors spread among the troops and the population at large of treason in high places: the empress, German by origin, was accused of betraying military secrets to the enemy. To compound the government's troubles, the cities experienced serious inflation, while the deterioration of rail transport caused shortages of food and fuel, especially in Petrograd (as Saint Petersburg had been renamed on the outbreak of the war). The combination of bad news from the front, political disaffection, and economic distress in the urban areas (the countryside was quiet, benefiting from higher prices on foodstuffs) created by October 1916 a revolutionary situation.

The Russian Revolution of 1917 may be said to have begun in November of the preceding year, when the government came under intense assault from liberal and conservative Duma deputies for its conduct of the war. The leader of the liberals, Paul Miliukov, virtually accused the government of treason. These attacks emanating from the highest political circles made the country ungovernable; the conviction spread that drastic change had to come. The tsar, a fatalist by nature, did nothing to reassert his authority.

The spark that set off the revolution was a mutiny, in early March 1917, of the Petrograd garrison. It consisted of older peasant draftees who felt they should have been exempt from military duty and rioted when ordered to fire at unruly civilian crowds. The generals, afraid of the mutiny spreading to the front, persuaded Nicholas to abdicate in order to save Russia from defeat. An ardent patriot, he followed their advice and on March 15 stepped down.

Following the tsar's abdication, power was assumed by a committee of Duma deputies, which called itself the Provisional Government. Concurrently with its formation, socialist intellectuals convened in Petrograd a *soviet*, or council of worker and soldier deputies. The soviet was to serve as a watchdog of the 'bourgeois' Provisional Government to ensure that it did not pursue reactionary policies. During the next seven months, Russia was governed – or rather misgoverned – by a regime of dual power, under which the soviets subverted the authority of the administration without assuming responsibility for the consequences. The socialist intellectuals running the soviet emasculated the army by reducing the authority of the officers, whom they regarded as a potentially counterrevolutionary force. Yet at the same time they insisted on the war being waged until victory.

The Provisional Government promised to convene without delay a Constituent Assembly to give the country a new republican administration; but, preoccupied with more urgent tasks, it kept postponing elections to it. It also kept deferring agrarian reform. Impatient peasants now attacked private estates while soldiers began to desert the front, eager to reach home in time to share in the anticipated repartition of land. The national minorities began to clamor for self-government and, in a few cases, for full sovereignty. And all this time, the Provisional Government insisted on pursuing a war that was losing support at home. The country, whose unity for centuries had been provided by state authority rather than social cohesion, slid into anarchy.

This gave Lenin his chance. In early 1917, he was living in Switzerland. On receipt of news of the March revolution, he cabled his lieutenants in Russia to distrust the Provisional Government, avoid alliances with the other socialist parties, and arm the workers. He burned with impatience to return home and take charge of the revolution.

The Germans and Austrians, bogged down on the western front in a seemingly interminable war of attrition, kept a close eye on Russian émigrés like Lenin who opposed the war. Lenin approached the German embassy in Switzerland for assistance in returning to Russia. Berlin not only offered him and other socialist émigrés safe passage through Germany but advanced him money with which to rebuild his party once he reached home. Lenin, who could not care less where money came from as long as it served his purposes, accepted the offer. Using intermediaries and exercising great caution, for the next year and a half he placed himself on the German payroll.

Immediately upon arriving in Petrograd, Lenin launched an uncompromising assault on the government, calling for its overthrow: it was not to be given the opportunity to establish in Russia a 'bourgeois' regime, as the Mensheviks and most of Lenin's own followers wanted. In July 1917, the Bolsheviks staged a halfhearted coup d'état, which the government quashed by releasing some of the intelligence it had on Lenin's dealings with the Germans. Orders went out for the arrest of Lenin and other leading Bolsheviks, including Leon Trotsky, who had recently joined the party. Trotsky went to prison, but Lenin escaped to Finland and remained there in hiding until the eve of his party's coup in November.

Lenin's following was small, but it was well organized and followed orders issued by the Central Committee. No other party had anything like it: the Socialists-Revolutionaries, who were far more popular with the population, especially the peasantry, had a loose structure that did not give them the capacity to mobilize their following. The same held true of the Mensheviks and the liberal Constitutional Democrats. Furthermore, no politician of note, apart from Lenin, wanted to take power and assume responsibility for governing a seemingly ungovernable country. Lenin, who had been preparing for this moment all his adult life, watched the unfolding situation carefully, awaiting the right moment to strike.

The moment came in the late summer, when Alexander Kerensky, the country's nominal but ineffective dictator, quarreled with General Lavr Kornilov, the commander in chief of Russia's armies, accusing him, unjustly, of planning a military putsch. By this irresponsible action, Kerensky lost support of the army, which he needed in the event of another Bolshevik attempt to seize power. At the same time he bolstered the Bolsheviks by releasing them from prison and giving them arms to help stop Kornilov's alleged coup. In the elections to the soviets held the next month, the Bolsheviks scored impressive gains, which signaled to Lenin that the time had come for another and decisive blow. The resolution to seize power was taken at a clandestine meeting of the Bolshevik leaders held on the night of October 23–24, 1917. Lenin had to overcome a great deal of reluctance from his lieutenants, who feared a repetition of the July fiasco.

The coup took place on November 7 when pro-Bolshevik units took over all the strategic points in the capital without firing a shot. There was some fighting in Moscow, but in the rest of the country the transition proceeded quite smoothly. Lenin later said that taking power in Russia was as easy as 'lifting a feather.' The reason was that he had cleverly camouflaged the seizure of power by himself and his party as the transfer of 'all power to the soviets,' which slogan promised grassroots democracy rather than dictatorship. Even Lenin's socialist rivals, who suspected his intentions, were not terribly upset, convinced that a Bolshevik one-party dictatorship could not possibly last and would soon yield to a socialist coalition. They preferred to let him exercise power for a while rather than unleash a civil war that would only benefit the 'counter-revolution.'

As it turned out, the Bolsheviks would stay in power for seventy-four years. Communism thus did not come to Russia as the result of a popular uprising: it was imposed on her from above by a small minority hiding behind democratic slogans. This salient fact was to determine its course.

Viewing the Bolsheviks' power seizure from the perspective of history, one can only marvel at their audacity. None of the leading Bolsheviks had experience in administering anything, and yet they were about to assume responsibility for governing the world's largest country. Nor, lacking business experience, did they shy from promptly nationalizing and hence assuming responsibility for managing the world's fifth-largest economy. They saw in the overwhelming majority of Russia's citizens – the bourgeoisie and the landowners as a matter of principle and most of the peasantry and intelligentsia as a matter of fact – class enemies of the industrial workers, whom they claimed to represent. These workers constituted a small proportion of Russia's population – at best 1 or 2 percent – and of this minority only a minuscule number followed the Bolsheviks: on the eve of the November coup, only 5.3 percent of industrial workers belonged to the Bolshevik party.[2] This meant that the new regime had no alternative but to turn into a dictatorship – a dictatorship not of the proletariat but over the proletariat and all the other classes. The dictatorship, which in time evolved into a totalitarian regime, was thus necessitated by the very nature of the Bolshevik takeover. As long as they wanted to stay in power, the Communists had to rule despotically and violently; they could never afford to relax their authority. The principle held true of every Communist regime that followed.

Lenin realized this and felt no qualms about imposing a ruthless despotism. He defined 'dictatorship' of any kind, including that of the 'proletariat,' as 'power that is limited by nothing, by no laws, that is restrained by absolutely no rules, that rests directly on coercion.'[3] He was quite prepared to resort to unlimited terror to destroy his opponents and cow the rest of the population. He did so in part because he was indifferent to human lives, but in part because the study of history had persuaded him that all past social revolutions had failed by stopping halfway and allowing their class enemies to survive and regroup. Violence – total and merciless (one of his favorite adjectives) – had to clear the ground for the new order. But he also believed that such violence would have to be of short duration: he once cited Machiavelli to the effect 'that if it is necessary to resort to certain brutalities for the sake of realizing a certain political goal, they must be carried out in the most energetic fashion and in the briefest possible time because the masses will not tolerate prolonged application of brutality.' Contrary to his expectations, these brutal-ities became a permanent feature of his regime. As Thomas Hobbes put it, if there is no agreement on trumps, clubs are trump.

Lenin's decisiveness and energy contrasted vividly with the helplessness of the overthrown Provisional Government. He authorized elections to the Constituent Assembly, which had been delayed for so long. His party received 24 percent of the national vote, while the rival Socialists-Revolutionaries gained more than twice that number. This did not in the least bother him: declaring that the workers and soldiers voted in large numbers for his party, he allowed the assembly to meet for one day and then dissolved it. The government that he set up, called the Council of People's Commissars, consisted exclusively of Bolsheviks. It was essentially an administrative facade that implemented orders from the Bolshevik Party. He abolished all legal procedures, turning justice over to Revolutionary Tribunals headed by untrained but 'class-conscious' laymen and the newly established secret police, called the Cheka. The terror began almost from the day he seized power.

Aware that to establish a solid political base and carry out his revolutionary program he needed time, in March 1918 Lenin had his lieutenants sign at Brest-Litovsk a highly unpopular peace treaty with the Germans, Austrians, Turks, and Bulgarians in which he surrendered vast territories.

And he unleashed a civil war in Russia as a prelude to the worldwide revolution, his ultimate objective. The Bolsheviks subsequently liked to blame the civil war that ravaged Russia for three years, claiming millions of lives, on Russian reactionaries and their foreign supporters. But, as we have noted, the transformation of the war from a conflict between nations to one between classes had been a central plank in the Bolshevik platform long before 1917. Trotsky admitted that much when he wrote, 'Soviet authority is organized civil war.' In fact, it may be said that the Bolsheviks seized power in Russia in order to make civil war.

Initially, in order to secure the support or at least the neutrality of peasants and workers, Lenin adopted anarchist slogans. He encouraged the peasants to appropriate and divide among themselves private land – not only that belonging to the state and landlords but also that of fellow peasants. A decree issued at the time of the coup nationalized all land but left untouched, for the time being, the plots tilled by the peasants themselves. He incited workers to take over factories, a syndicalist policy that had nothing in common with Marxism. But these were temporary measures that he intended to reverse as soon as he was firmly in power. For his ultimate purpose was to nationalize all of the country's human and material resources in order to subject the economy to a central plan.

The history of Soviet Russia between 1917 and 1920 need not detain us. Suffice it to say that the Communists – the name the Bolsheviks adopted in 1918 – won the civil war, in part because they controlled the populous center of the country, where the bulk of its industrial (and military) assets were located, in part because the Western powers extended to their opponents, known as 'Whites,' only halfhearted support. In the course of the civil war and soon after its conclusion, the regime reconquered most of the non-Russian borderlands – the Ukraine, the Caucasus, and Central Asia – which had previously separated themselves. These were merged with Soviet Russia to form, in 1924, the Union of Soviet Socialist Republics. All the territories of the new empire were ruled, in fact if not in theory, by the same Russian Communist Party with headquarters in Moscow. Its branches penetrated every segment of organized life, serving, to use a term coined by Mussolini, who would model his Fascist rule on Lenin's, as the 'capillary organization of the regime.' No organization, not even of the most innocuous kind, could escape the Communist Party's control. Thus emerged the first one-party state in history.

Except for retaining their grip on power, the Bolsheviks experienced setbacks in nearly all their endeavors. Life turned out to be very different from theory. But they would not admit they were wrong: whenever things did not turn out as desired, they did not compromise but instead intensified the violence. To admit to being wrong would threaten to unravel the whole theoretical foundation of their regime, since it claimed to be scientifically correct in all its parts.

First as concerns the state.

Among the many of Lenin's disappointments was the emergence of a huge, self-serving, and uncontrollable bureaucracy. According to Marxist doctrine, the state is nothing more than the servant of the class that owns the means of production; it has no interests of its own. This belief showed remarkable ignorance of political history since there exists a great deal of evidence that, from the time of the pharaohs, state officials looked after themselves and formed an interest group in many instances more influential than the propertied class. Lenin was appalled by the rapid growth of the Soviet bureaucracy, which his own policies had necessitated. For as the Communist Party, through the state, took charge of the entire organized life of the country, nationalizing large and small industries, retail and wholesale trade, transport and services, educational and other institutions, the officialdom that replaced the private owners and their managers expanded by leaps and bounds. Suffice it to say that the organization in charge of the country's industry, the Supreme Council of the National Economy, employed in 1921 nearly one quarter of a million officials, and this at a time when industrial productivity had dropped to below one-fifth of its 1913 level. By 1928, the party and state bureaucracy came to number 4 million.

The great majority of those who had joined the ranks of Soviet functionaries – many of them holdovers from the old regime – did so because a government job assured them a modicum of security and livelihood. Before long, they came to constitute a caste that placed its collective interests above not only those of the population at large but those of the Communist cause that they nominally served.

The first to realize the potential uses of the Soviet bureaucracy as an instrument for shoring up his personal position in the party was Joseph Stalin. A semieducated Georgian who in his youth had dropped out of religious seminary and joined the Bolsheviks, he had gained Lenin's confidence by his devotion to him as well as by displaying outstanding administrative talents. Unlike Trotsky and the other Communist leaders, such as Lev Kamenev and Grigorii Zinoviev, Stalin never questioned Lenin's judgment; and while they wrote pamphlets and delivered speeches, he quietly supervised the burgeoning army of functionaries. Lenin advanced him ahead of his more intellectual associates and in 1922 had him appointed the party's general secretary, which gave Stalin control of the party's cadres.

From the outset, Stalin used his office to promote Communists who owed him personal loyalty and on whom he could rely in the struggle for party leadership likely to break out before long because of Lenin's failing health. It is he who created the institution of the *nomenklatura:* registers of Communist officials eligible for important executive appointments and rewarded with such privileges as access to special food stores, hospitals, resorts, and even tailors and cemeteries. The policy of creating a privileged elite sustained the Communist regime for the next seventy years by ensconcing an administrative class with a vital interest in the regime's survival. But, by the same token, it ensured that the Communist ideal of social equality would remain an empty slogan.

No less galling were the Bolsheviks' disappointments with managing the economy. Socialist literature had assured them that capitalism, driven by profit, was inherently much less efficient than an economy monopolized by the state. They believed that the bigger an enterprise, the better it functioned. They further believed that it was possible to run an economy without resort to money.

All these assumptions turned out to be wrong. Attempts to impose a central plan on the national economy proved futile.

Mismanagement of factories, first by workers and then by Communist functionaries who replaced them, drastically lowered productivity. The effort, enforced by the Cheka, to stop private trade also failed in its purpose, as producers and middlemen found ways to circumvent it; the free market, which the Communists saw as the quintessence of capitalism and which they were determined to liquidate, did not vanish but shifted underground. Before long, the shadow economy outstripped the official Soviet one. The hyperinflation that the government deliberately launched by flooding the country with banknotes did achieve its aim of destroying savings: by 1923, prices in the Soviet Union had increased 100 million times over those of 1917. But the abandonment of money made it impossible to keep a proper budget or calculate transactions between Soviet enterprises.

The net result of such amateurish management, aggravated by the civil war, was a catastrophic drop of all productive indices. Overall large-scale industrial production in 1920 was 18 percent of what it had been in 1913; the output of coal dropped to 27 percent and iron to 2.4 percent. The number of employed industrial workers in 1921 was less than one-half of what it had been in 1918; their living standard fell to one-third of its prewar level.[4] A Communist specialist described what happened to the Soviet economy between 1917 and 1920 as a calamity 'unparalleled in the history of mankind.'[5]

When confronted with such failures, Lenin's instinct was to resort to the firing squad. Isaac Steinberg, a Left Socialist Revolutionary who for a while served as the Communist commissar of justice, describes a meeting of the Council of People's Commissars in February 1918. Lenin had presented the draft

45

of a decree, 'The Socialist Fatherland in Danger!,' which contained a clause calling for the execution 'on the spot,' i.e., without trial, of a broad category of criminals loosely defined as 'enemy agents, speculators, burglars, hooligans, counter-revolutionary agitators, [and] German spies.' Steinberg objected to the decree on the grounds that it contained a 'cruel threat… with far-reaching terroristic potentialities.'

> Lenin resented my opposition in the name of revolutionary justice. So I called out in exasperation, 'Then why do we bother with a Commissariat of Justice? Let's call it frankly the *Commissariat for Social Extermination* and be done with it!' Lenin's face suddenly brightened and he replied, 'Well put… that's exactly what it should be… but we can't say that.'[6]

The most tragic aspect of the economic disaster was the decline in food production.

As stated above, the Communists, in common with other Marxists, regarded the peasantry as a petit bourgeois class and, as such, a sworn enemy of industrial labor – this despite the fact that in Russia the majority of industrial workers came from the village and maintained close links to it. The Communists declared war on the rural population for two purposes: to extract food for the cities and the Red Army and to insinuate their authority into the countryside, which remained largely unaffected by the Bolshevik coup.

In the summer of 1918, Moscow launched a campaign to extract grain from the villages, which the peasants were unwilling to sell to the government at unrealistically low fixed prices. It created in the villages 'Committees of the Poor,' a kind of rural fifth column expected, in exchange for a share of the hoard, to collaborate with the government against the wealthier peasants (the kulaks), who were suspected of hoarding food. Concurrently, Moscow sent into the countryside detachments of armed urban hoodlums to collect the 'surplus.' The result was pitched battles between peasants, many of them demobilized soldiers, and food detachments. Much of the country was engulfed in a civil war, more vicious than that pitting the Red Army against the Whites. Lenin, labeling as a kulak any peasant who resisted Soviet authority, fulminated and called for large-scale pogroms. The following are two examples of his directives, both dating from August 1918, the first one from a speech he delivered to workers, the second from a secret order he sent to Communist officials in the Penza province:

> The kulak insanely detests Soviet authority and is ready to suffocate, to carve up hundreds of thousands of workers. ... Either the kulak will cut up a boundless number of workers, or the workers will mercilessly crush the uprising of the thievish minority of the people against the power of the toilers... The kulaks are the most beastly, the coarsest, the most savage exploiters... These bloodsuckers have waxed rich during the war on the people's want... These spiders have grown fat at the expense of peasants, impoverished by the war, of hungry workers. These leeches have drunk the blood of toilers, growing the richer the more the worker starved in the cities and factories. These vampires have gathered and continue to gather in their hands the lands of the landlords, enslaving, time and again, the poor peasants. Merciless war against these kulaks! Death to them.[7]

> Comrades! The uprising of the five kulak districts should be

mercilessly suppressed. The interests of the *entire* revolution require this because now 'the last decisive battle' with the kulaks is under way *everywhere.* One must give an example.

1) Hang (hang without fail, so *the people see*) *no fewer than one hundred* known kulaks, rich men, bloodsuckers.

2) Publish their names.

3) Take from them *all* the grain.

4) Designate hostages – as per yesterday's telegram. Do it in such a way that for hundreds of versts [kilometers] around the people will see, tremble, know, shout: *they are strangling* and will strangle to death the bloodsucker kulaks.

Telegraph receipt and *implementation.*

Yours. Lenin.

Find some *truly hard* people.[8]

One response of the peasants, rich and poor alike, to this terror was to curtail the sown acreage so as to reduce the 'surplus' subject to confiscation. At the same time, shortages of draft horses, mobilized for the civil war, lowered yields. As a consequence, cereal grain harvests declined from 78.2 million tons in 1913 to 48.2 million in 1920.

In early 1921, all the problems that Lenin's government had brought on itself through its efforts to impose Communism on what, by its own definition, was an overwhelmingly counter-revolutionary country came to a head. In January, the naval base at Kronshtadt, off Petrograd, previously a bastion of Bolshevism, mutinied, issuing appeals to the nation to end the Communist tyranny. Concurrently, large-scale strikes broke out in Petrograd to protest against food shortages. A major peasant rebellion was under way in the Tambov province.

Lenin did not hesitate to crush these acts of defiance by the most brutal military means, resorting even to the use of poison gas. But he reluctantly concluded that force was not enough. In early 1921, he announced the introduction of the New Economic Policy (NEP), whose key provision was the abandonment of forcible exactions of food: the peasants were henceforth to pay a tax in kind and allowed to sell their surplus on the open market. The government also authorized a limited amount of trade and private manufacture of consumer goods. But it made certain to retain control of what it called 'the commanding heights' of the economy, namely basic industries, foreign trade, banking, means of communications, and transport.

These concessions came too late to avoid a frightful famine, the worst any European country had ever suffered until then. Triggered by a drought, it claimed 5.2 million lives, and would have been more devastating yet were it not for the help provided by the American Relief Administration headed by future U.S. president Herbert Hoover, which fed 25 million people.

Recovery under the NEP showed astonishing progress. By 1928, Russia's grain production reached levels not seen since 1913.

Many in and out of Russia believed that the NEP marked the abandonment of Communism. There was talk of a 'Russian Thermidor,' with reference to the events in France in 1794 that had led to the fall and execution of Jacobin leaders. But the analogy was inappropriate: for one, the Russian Jacobins remained firmly in the saddle; for another, they viewed their concessions as merely a breathing spell. And so they turned out to be.

The Bolsheviks seized power in Russia only because it was a target of opportunity. They had no intention of staying within its borders, convinced that their revolution would be crushed by the combined forces of world capitalism unless it speedily spread to the industrial countries of the West. Lenin put the issue bluntly: 'We have always emphasized that one cannot achieve such a task as a socialist revolution in one country.'[9] In a speech delivered in 1920, he made the foreign dimension of the Russian Revolution unmistakably clear:

> [In November 1917] we knew that our victory will be a lasting victory only when our undertaking will conquer the whole world, because we had launched it exclusively counting on the world revolution.[10]

Thus it happened that the Communist government, which inside its own borders was exceedingly conservative, tolerating no initiatives from below, abroad, and only abroad, acted in a radical manner, stirring up the very masses whom it had silenced at home.

The attempt to spread Communism abroad began in earnest at the conclusion of World War I among the defeated Central Powers. In January 1919 Moscow instigated a revolt in Germany that was quickly quelled. The Communists had somewhat greater success in Hungary, where their government managed to stay in power for half of 1919 but only because of Soviet Russia's promise to defend Hungary from the invading Romanian armies. When Moscow failed to make good on this pledge, its proxy regime fell. Similar attempts elsewhere, such as Vienna, fizzled out almost before they got started.

Lenin's great disappointment with spreading Communism

abroad occurred in the summer of 1920. In April of that year, Poland, eager to forestall the reemergence of a strong and imperialist Russia, had made common cause with Ukrainian nationalists and invaded the Soviet Ukraine with the aim of detaching it from Russia. The invasion failed to ignite an uprising in the Ukraine, and the Polish armies soon found themselves in full retreat.

As the Red Army approached the borders of ethnic Poland, the Politburo, the directing organ of the Communist Party, had to decide whether to stop or to continue advancing westward. Opinions were divided but Lenin insisted on offensive operations, and as by now was always the case, he had his way. He felt certain that both Germany and England were ripe for revolution, which the appearance of Communist armed forces on their borders would help ignite. In the summer of 1920, the Red Army, accompanied by Soviet commissars of Polish origin, entered Poland. It broadcast appeals calling on Polish workers and peasants to seize properties of the bourgeois and landlords – slogans that had proven very effective in Russia. But the Poles of all classes rallied to defend newly won Polish sovereignty. In the battle for Warsaw, one of the decisive battles of modern history, they repulsed and scattered the Communist army.

Lenin could not conceal his bitterness at this outcome. 'In the Red Army the Poles saw enemies, not brothers and liberators,' he complained.

> They felt, thought and acted not in a social, revolutionary way, but as nationalists, as imperialists. The revolution in Poland on which we had counted did not take place. The workers and

peasants ... defended their class enemy, they let our brave Red soldiers starve, ambushed them and beat them to death."

One conclusion he drew from this experience was that the Red Army must never again be used abroad as an instrument of revolution. Instead, financial and other help should be extended to indigenous forces.

Another, even more important lesson Lenin drew from the Polish debacle was that the best chance for spreading revolution abroad was to instigate another world war. In this war, Soviet Russia would remain neutral and step in only once the belligerents had exhausted themselves. To this end, in 1921 Moscow initiated secret military cooperation with Germany.

III   *Stalin and After*

Lenin's health began to fail in May 1922, when he suffered his first stroke. Although attended to by a team of specialists from Germany, he showed no improvement and had to gradually give up his political responsibilities. In his last days he was haunted by a sense of failure: he was angry at his associates and, indeed, the Russian people for failing to measure up to the grand mission that history had assigned them.

In this mood, he looked for enemies who thwarted his designs. One day it was the intellectuals, who overwhelmingly rejected his dictatorship even though they did not engage in active subversion. In July 1922, he instructed Stalin 'decisively to "eradicate" all S[ocialists-] R[evolutionaries]... all of them – get out of Russia.... Arrest a few hundred and *without explaining* the motives – "Out you go, gentlemen!"' Acting on his orders, the police rounded up hundreds of economists, philosophers, and other scholars belonging to the Socialist-Revolutionary, Menshevik, and liberal parties, loaded them on ships, and sent them off into forced exile in western Europe.

Another day it was the Orthodox Church. In the spring of 1922, when Soviet Russia was in the throes of a famine, Lenin thought he had gained a unique opportunity to achieve two aims: to appropriate the church's wealth under the pretext of using it to feed the hungry and, in the likely event of encountering the church's resistance, to demonstrate to the population its heartlessness. In a memorandum to the Politburo he wrote:

> It is precisely now and only now, when in the starving regions people are eating human flesh, and hundreds if not thousands of corpses are littering the roads, that we can (and therefore must) carry out the confiscation of church valuables with the most savage and merciless energy...so as to secure for ourselves a fund of several hundred million gold rubles.[1]

The assets thus confiscated did not go for famine relief but for the needs of the Soviet state.

In March 1923 Lenin suffered a debilitating stroke that deprived him of speech. Eight months later he died. The party had made no provisions for his replacement. Since it owed no accountability to its subjects, it could maintain continuity only by co-optation. Into the gap stepped Secretary-General Joseph Stalin. Moderate in his public pronouncements and jovial in manner, giving no hint of his sadistic and paranoid personality, he had acquired considerable popularity among the party's rank and file. Thus in the (secret) ballot for the Party's Central Committee held in March 1919, he (along with Nicholas Bukharin) had gathered more votes than any other candidate except Lenin, far more than the better known Trotsky, widely regarded as Lenin's heir apparent.

Stalin first teamed up with Kamenev and Zinoviev, members of the triumvirate that had run the party during Lenin's illness, to be rid of their common rival, Trotsky. By slander, intimidation of his supporters, and similar underhanded methods they stripped Trotsky of his posts, expelled him from the party, and then exiled him, first to Central Asia and finally, in 1929, abroad, where, in 1940, Stalin had him murdered. Stalin next turned on Kamenev and Zinoviev, whom he had removed from the Politburo. His victims' ability to defend themselves against fabricated accusations was fatally weakened by their acceptance of the principle that 'the party is always right.'

Although in his exile Trotsky liked to depict himself as Lenin's favorite and Stalin as someone whom Lenin despised, in fact the secretary-general was a faithful disciple and the rightful heir of Soviet Russia's founder. Within a year or two of Lenin's death he was clearly the party's boss: having solidified his power, he was ready to resume the drive for Communism interrupted in 1921 by the introduction of the NEP. He had three related objectives: to build a powerful industrial base, to collectivize agriculture, and to impose on the nation complete conformity. These ambitious objectives provoked a crisis in the country, which was finally recovering from the turmoils of World War I, revolution, and civil war. But this did not trouble Stalin, because Communist regimes thrived on crises.

> Crisis alone permitted the authorities to demand – and obtain – total submission and all necessary sacrifices from its citizens. The system needed sacrifices and sacrificial victims for the good of the cause and the happiness of future generations. Crises enabled the system in this way to build a bridge from the fictional world of utopian programs to the world of reality.[2]

When, following Stalin's death, his successors would opt for stability, decay would set in because the citizens no longer saw the rationale for the sacrifices demanded of them.

The subversion of the NEP got under way in December 1925, when the party congress resolved to launch an ambitious program of forced industrialization. And industrialization, for reasons that will be spelled out below, implied collectivization of agriculture. Since both objectives called for immense hardships, the voices of dissent had to be silenced. Thus Stalinism was of a piece and could survive only as long as all its elements were intact.

To begin with industrialization: it was a Marxist-Leninist axiom that a socialist society must rest on an industrial base, and since Russia's industries were still relatively rudimentary it was necessary to construct the base virtually from scratch. When the effort was completed, the Soviet Union would acquire a world-class economy and a sizable working class, enabling it to confront its capitalist rivals on equal terms. That much was beyond dispute, though the pace of industrialization led to disagreements at the party's highest levels, until Stalin silenced them, imposing breakneck speed regardless of the human cost.

But there was yet another reason for forced industrialization, one almost never mentioned at the time and rarely since, and that was preparation for another world war. In December 1927 Stalin announced that the 'imperialists' were arming for a new war and military intervention against the USSR. To meet this (imaginary) threat, the Soviet Union required a formidable defense industry. Indeed, the entire Soviet industrial buildup was from the beginning geared to military needs.

The first Five-Year Plan, ratified in 1929, which subjected the entire national economy to central management, emphasized capital goods: steel and iron, coal, oil, heavy machinery. The central planning organization set completely unrealistic production goals, made still more unattainable by Stalin's order, issued in 1931, that the plan be completed in three years. By 1932, the principal industrial indicators, which were to have been tripled, had actually doubled. So had the industrial labor force, which had expanded from 3 to 6.4 million.

The government managed to arouse enthusiasm for the 'construction of socialism' by promising that it would significantly improve living standards. But this was a carrot that forever eluded the consumer. In reality, living standards declined precipitously because financing the industrialization drive called for reducing wages to a minimum. In 1933, workers' real earnings sank to about one-tenth of what they had been on the eve of the industrial drive (1926–27). According to Alec Nove, a specialist on the Soviet economy, '1933 was the culmination of the most precipitous peacetime decline in living standards known in recorded history.'[3]

To spur productivity, Stalin appealed to traditional capitalist methods of motivation. In 1931, he assailed the principle of 'egalitarianism,' which called for workers to be paid identical wages regardless of competence, as an 'ultra-left' notion. It meant, he went on to explain, that the unqualified worker had no incentive to acquire skills, while the skilled worker moved from job to job until he found one where his talents were properly rewarded; both hurt productivity. Accordingly, the new wage scale drew great distinctions between the least and the most skilled workers.

The capital for the industrialization drive came from various sources, including the printing of banknotes, the proceeds of a turnover tax, and exports of food and even artworks.

But the bulk of it was extracted from the peasantry, which, seven decades after emancipation, was effectively re-enserfed. A firm decision to proceed with 'mass collectivization' came in mid-1929. In Stalin's words, it had become necessary to industrialize the country with the help of internal accumulation. By this was meant that the peasants would supply the food for the industrial labor force, cities, and armed forces at rock-bottom prices. But the propaganda accompanying collectivization placed emphasis on the elimination of rural 'exploiters,' to divert attention from the fact that by far the most numerous victims of collectivization were ordinary peasants.

Collectivization entailed two processes. One was the 'liquidation of the kulaks as a class,' in other words, as human beings; the other, the destruction of peasant communes as well as of any independence of the peasantry. The peasants were herded into collective farms (kolkhozy), where they labored not for themselves but for the state. It was an unprecedented revolution from above, involving the relegation of three-quarters of the country's population to the status of government chattel.

The kulaks – the term covered better-off peasants as well as those who actively resisted collectivization – had all their belongings confiscated and were deported either to hard-labor camps or, along with their families, into Siberian exile. According to official records, in 1930 and 1931, 1,803,392 people suffered one or the other of these punishments. It is estimated that as many as 30 percent of those who eluded execution perished from cold and hunger.[4] Of the survivors, an estimated 400,000 managed, in time, to escape and find a precarious home in the cities and industrial centers.

The 'middle' and 'poor' peasants also lost all they had, including their implements and livestock – or what was left of the latter after they had slaughtered rather than surrender it; these properties were turned over to the collective farm. The collectivized peasants were required to work a designated number of days per year for minimal wages in money and grain to fulfill the delivery norms imposed by the state; the state paid the farms kopecks and resold the grain to consumers as flour or bread for rubles, earning a profit of several hundred percent. Farmers who failed to meet these norms went hungry. And those who out of desperation stole food were treated as dangerous criminals: a notorious decree of August 1932 provided for the death penalty or ten years of hard labor for 'any theft or damage of socialist [read: Communist Party] property,' which term covered stealing a few stalks of grain. Under this law, in the sixteen months that followed, over 125,000 peasants were sentenced, 5,400 to death.[5] Since the only produce the peasants received from the collective farm was grain, the government in 1935 allowed kolkhoz farmers to cultivate private garden plots, averaging one acre per family, where they could grow fruits and vegetables for their own consumption and for sale at state-supervised collective-farm markets. They were also permitted to keep cows and smaller domestic animals (but no horses). These private holdings contributed a great deal of the country's produce and meat, quite out of proportion to their size.

Collectivization degraded the peasant more than did pre-1861 serfdom, since as a serf he had owned (in practice, if not in theory) his crops and livestock. His new status was that of a slave laborer who received the bare minimum of subsistence: for backbreaking work in 1935 a peasant household earned from the kolkhoz 247 rubles a year, just enough to purchase one pair of shoes.[6]

Stalin liked to pretend that collectivization was carried out voluntarily, but in fact the government resorted to extreme violence. He told Churchill that the collectivization campaign, which lasted some three years, had been more 'stressful' than World War II. If it was so hard on him, one can imagine how much harder it was on his victims. To break the resistance of the peasants in the Ukraine, the North Caucasus, and Kazakhstan, Stalin inflicted on these areas in 1932–33 an artificial famine, shipping out all the food from entire districts and deploying the army to prevent the starving peasants from migrating in search of nourishment. It is estimated that between 6 and 7 million people perished in this man-made catastrophe.[7] To overcome the resistance of the nomadic Kazakhs in Central Asia, the regime resorted to extraordinary brutality: it is believed that as much as one-third of the Kazakh population perished in the process.[8]

Collectivization achieved its short-term objective, which was to finance a good part of the industrialization drive; in effect, the peasants' food was confiscated and distributed to the cities and industrial centers. In the long run, its consequences were catastrophic: it ruined Russian agriculture, first by deporting the most enterprising farmers, and secondly by depriving the kolkhoz peasant of a stake in the land, the crops of which no longer belonged to him. Russia, which before the revolution had been one of the world's leading cereal exporters, henceforth could barely feed herself.

The worst was over by 1934–35, when food rationing was abolished and Stalin proclaimed that 'life has become more joyous, comrades, life has become gayer.' Not for long, however: the regime needed another crisis to justify its despotic powers. It also needed enemies. As Fidel Castro, the leader of Communist Cuba, would explain with a frankness that his Russian mentors preferred to avoid: 'The revolution needs the enemy… The revolution needs for its development its antithesis, which is the counterrevolution.'[9] And if enemies were lacking, they had to be fabricated.

In 1934 a prominent Bolshevik, Sergei Kirov, the party boss of Leningrad, was assassinated under mysterious conditions; circumstantial evidence points to Stalin as the instigator of the murder. A staunch Stalinist – shortly before being murdered, he had hailed Stalin as the 'great strategist of the liberation of the toilers of our country and the entire world' – Kirov was gaining too much popularity in party ranks for Stalin's comfort. His assassination brought Stalin two advantages: it rid him of a potential rival and provided a rationale for instigating a vast campaign against alleged anti-Soviet conspirators, in the course of which he would eliminate the top cadres he had inherited from Lenin. The so-called purges of the 1930s were a terror campaign that in indiscriminate ferocity and number of victims had no parallel in world history. It was minutely supervised by Stalin himself, whose instructions to local authorities focused on one method: beat them until they confess to crimes they have not committed.

What this injunction meant in practice we are able to learn from a letter sent to Stalin's close associate Vyacheslav Molotov by one of the terror's innumerable victims, Vsevolod Meyerhold. A leading Russian theatrical producer and a Communist since the early years of the regime, Meyerhold was declared, for no apparent reason, an 'enemy of the people' and arrested in 1939. He wrote:

When the investigators began to apply to me physical methods they beat me, a sick, old man of sixty-five. They placed me on the floor, face down; they beat me with a rubber whip on my heels and back. When I sat on a bench, they used the same rubber whip to beat me from above, with great force. In the days that followed, when these parts of my legs hemorrhaged profusely, they again beat these red-blue-yellow blood-filled places with the same rubber whip and the pain was such that it seemed they were pouring on these sick, sore areas intensely boiling water, and I screamed and cried from pain. They beat my back with this rubber; they beat me by hand on the face, swinging from above.... They combined this with a so-called 'psychic attack.' The one and the other aroused in me such monstrous fear that my personality was stripped to its very roots.... Lying on the floor with my face down, I twisted, contorted, and howled like a dog whom its owner beats with a lash ...

I lay down on my cot and fell asleep only in order an hour later to be led again to the interrogation, which previously had lasted eighteen hours, awakened by groans and by having tossed on the cot like a sick man dying of fever. 'Death (yes, of course!), death is easier than this!' is what one person under investigation said

to himself. I, too, told myself this. And I began to slander myself
in the hope that they would lead me to the scaffold...[10]

After he had duly incriminated himself, the authorities obliged
and executed Meyerhold.

The Great Terror struck at the party membership as well as
ordinary citizens. At its height, in 1937 and 1938, at least one
and a half million people, the vast majority of them innocent
of any wrongdoing even by Communist criteria, were hauled
before troikas, tribunals made up of the first secretary of the
regional party, the procurator, and the local security police
chief. After summary proceedings often lasting no more than a
few minutes and from which there was no appeal, the defen-
dant would be sentenced to death, hard labor, or exile.
Abstention from politics offered no security, nor did whole-
hearted commitment to the regime. At the pinnacle of the
Great Terror, the Politburo issued 'quotas' to the police authorities, instructing them as to what percentage of the population
in their district was to be shot and what percentage sent to
camps. For example, on June 2, 1937, it set a quota of 35,000
persons to be 'repressed' in Moscow city and Moscow province,
of which number 5,000 were to be shot.[11] One month later, the
Politburo provided each region with quotas of persons to be
'rounded up' nationwide; 70,000 of them were to be executed
without trial.[12] A high proportion of the victims of the Great
Terror were persons with a higher education considered
difficult to control and prone to engage in 'sabotage.'

How much the purge affected the party elite can be seen
from the fact that of the 139 members and candidate members
of the Central Committee elected at the Seventeenth Party

Congress in 1934, 70 percent were executed.[13] All of Lenin's close associates, including Zinoviev and Kamenev, suffered arrest and torture and, once physically and mentally crushed, were forced to stand staged 'trials' in which they confessed to the most heinous crimes, including espionage, terrorist acts, and attempts to restore 'capitalism'; after this they were either executed or sent to hard-labor camps, from which few emerged alive. In his so-called 'Testament,' Lenin listed six leading Communists as his potential successors; all but one – Stalin – perished. Dmitrii Volkogonov, a Soviet general turned historian, was, in his own words, 'deeply shaken' when he found in the archive thirty lists dating from a single day, December 12, 1938. The lists carried the names of some 5,000 people whose death warrants Stalin had signed before they had even been nominally tried, following which he went to his private Kremlin movie theater to enjoy two films, one of them a comedy called *Merry Fellows*.[14]

In one way or another, most of the population was compelled to participate in this destructive orgy by informing on their friends and acquaintances; failure to report 'subversive' talk was tantamount to subversion. In this atmosphere, there was no room for loyalty or truthfulness. A Russian joke quite realistically defined a decent Soviet citizen as someone who acted like a swine but did not enjoy it.

The massacres of 1937–38 virtually wiped out the ranks of 'old Bolsheviks,' whose place was taken by newcomers. In 1939, 80.5 percent of the executive personnel of the Soviet Union's Communist Party had joined since Lenin's death.[15] From their ranks came the top officials of the party and government, the so-called *nomenklatura*, which not only monopolized all positions of authority but enjoyed unique privileges, forming a new exploiting class. Membership of it guaranteed permanent status and became de facto hereditary. When the Soviet Union collapsed, the *nomenklatura* numbered some 750,000 members – with their families, around 3 million persons, or 1.5 percent of the population, approximately the proportion of service nobles under tsarism in the eighteenth century. And the favors it enjoyed resembled those of the magnates of that age. In the words of a member of that elite:

> the nomenklatura is on another planet. It's Mars. It's not simply a matter of good cars or apartments. It's the continuous satisfaction of your own whims, the way an army of boot-lickers allows you to work painlessly for hours. All the little apparatchiks are ready to do everything for you. Your every wish is fulfilled. You can go to the theater on a whim, you can fly to Japan from your hunting lodge. It's a life in which everything flows easily.... You are like a king: just point your finger and it is done.[16]

The rank and file of the party, the 'boot-lickers,' whose numbers had swollen immensely under Stalin, served this elite corps as attendants.

The Red Army did not escape the terror: of its five marshals, three suffered 'liquidation'; of the army's fifteen generals, thirteen perished; of nine navy admirals, only one survived. Foreign Communists who had sought refuge in the Soviet Union were also decimated. The clergy suffered devastating losses: in 1937–38, 165,200 churchmen were arrested for the crime of practicing their religion, and of that number, 106,800 were shot.[17] Nearly all the places of worship were closed.

The terror machine did not spare its own managers. Nikolai Ezhov, Stalin's Himmler, who administered the mass murders as head of the NKVD between 1936 and 1938, for some reason fell afoul of his master. Stalin had him removed from office, arrested, and thrown into the bloody cauldron.

Ordinary citizens were imprisoned and disappeared because of a chance remark or denunciation by personal enemies. A pathological fear and suspicion gripped the population, from which even the highest functionaries were not exempt. Thus Nikolai Bulganin, who had served under Stalin as deputy prime minister of the USSR, told Nikita Khrushchev that at times one would be invited by Stalin as a friend: 'And, when he sits with Stalin, he does not know where he will be sent next – home or to jail.' Andrei Gromyko, minister of foreign affairs and Stalin's loyal assistant, related that under Stalin two or more members of the Politburo never rode in the same car, out of fear of being suspected of conspiracy. The fear and suspicion survived Stalin, having become an intrinsic part of the system. Mikhail Gorbachev, the last leader of the Soviet Union, would recall that when he invited his patron and neighbor Iurii Andropov, then head of the KGB, to dinner, Andropov advised him, for his own good, to drop the idea or 'there would be all kinds of loose talk – who, where, why, what was said.'

According to evidence released from secret archives since the dissolution of the Soviet Union (which some experts consider understated), during 1937 and 1938, when the Great Terror was at its height, the security organs detained for alleged 'anti-Soviet activities' 1,548,366 persons, of whom 681,692 were shot – an average of 1,000 executions a day. The majority of the survivors ended up in hard-labor camps.[18] (For comparison, the tsarist regime between 1825 and 1910 executed for political crimes 3,932 persons.) In 1941, when Germany invaded the USSR, camps run by the Gulag, their main administrative body, held 2,350,000 inmates, or 1.4 percent of the country's population.[19] The slave laborers performed important economic functions, being employed on large construction projects and forced to cut timber in the far north. No one responsible for these crimes against innocent people was tried after the Soviet Union had collapsed; indeed, they did not even suffer exposure or moral opprobrium but continued to lead normal lives.

Censuses revealed that between 1932 and 1939 – that is, after collectivization but before World War II – the population of the Soviet Union decreased by 9 to 10 million people.[20]

This orgy of destruction defied rational explanation. Black humor told of a new prisoner arriving at a hard-labor camp. Asked how long a term he had drawn, he replies, 'Twenty-five years.' 'For what?' 'For nothing.' 'Impossible,' he is told. 'For nothing you get ten years.'

If one wonders how any government could inflict such devastation on its own people, it must be borne in mind that for Communist revolutionaries, in Russia and elsewhere, human beings such as they were represented a travesty of what humans could, should, and had to become. This view was embedded in Marxism. Marx once wrote that

> the present generation resembles the Jews whom Moses led through the wilderness. It must not only conquer a new world, it must also *perish* in order to make room for the people who are fit for a new world.[21]

While neither Marx nor Engels encouraged their followers to commit mass murder, they were quite prepared to sacrifice the living for generations yet unborn.

And indeed it was well worth waiting for them, because the 'new man' under Communism would be unlike any creature ever known. Trotsky thus depicted him in his *Literature and Revolution*:

> Man will, at last, begin to harmonize himself in earnest.... He will want to master first the semi-conscious and then also the unconscious processes of his own organism: breathing, the circulation of blood, digestion, reproduction, and, within the necessary limits, subordinate them to the control of reason and will.... The human species, the sluggish *Homo sapiens*, will once again enter the state of radical reconstruction and become in his own hands the object of the most complex methods of artificial se-lection and psychophysical training...Man will make it his goal...to create a higher sociobiological type, a superman, if you will...Man will become incomparably stronger, wiser, more subtle. His body will become more harmonious, his movements more rhythmic, his voice more melodious...The average human type will rise to the heights of an Aristotle, Goethe, Marx. And beyond this ridge, other peaks will emerge.

For such an ideal, was it not worth sacrificing the sorry specimens that populated the corrupt world? Seen from this perspective, existing humanity was debris, the refuse of a doomed world, and killing it off was a matter of no consequence.

The unprecedented destruction of lives was accompanied by a resolute drive against free speech designed to create the illusion of complete unanimity: along with bodies exterminated or incarcerated, minds, too, were dispossessed. Lenin himself showed no respect for the expression of views that differed from his own; his very first decree upon coming to power ordered the closing of the entire non-Bolshevik press. He was not strong enough as yet to enforce this measure, but in the summer of 1918 he did shut down not only all independent newspapers but also the entire nonparty periodical press. In 1922 he set up a central censorship bureau, called Glavlit. Nothing could appear in print or on the stage without its imprimatur.

Nevertheless, in the 1920s a certain amount of intellectual freedom was still tolerated. Early Soviet censorship, like tsarist censorship, was negative in nature in that it laid down what could not be published but did not attempt to tell authors what to write. In the 1930s this policy changed: censorship became positive as authors were instructed what they should and, indeed, had to write. All negative information about the country was suppressed – unless it suited the authorities to reveal some aspect of it. Travel abroad was limited to official personnel; for ordinary citizens any contacts with foreigners risked charges of espionage. No foreign publications, except pro-Communist ones, were distributed.

A fantastic uniformity descended on Soviet culture. 'Socialist realism' became the official aesthetic doctrine in 1932; it required writers and artists to treat the present 'as though it did not exist and the future as if it had already arrived.'[22] In consequence, what was printed, staged, filmed, or broadcast in no way corresponded to reality: it was a surreality. People adjusted to it by splitting, as it were, their minds and

69

personalities, creating a schizophrenic condition, on one level of which they knew the truth but repressed it, sharing it only with their closest family and friends, while on another they pretended to believe every word of official propaganda. This created a strain that made life in the Soviet Union exceedingly difficult to bear.

It also left a psychic legacy that outlasted Communism. Lying became a means of survival, and from lying to cheating was but a small step. Social ethics, which make possible a civil society, were shattered, and a regime that wanted everyone to sacrifice his private advantage to the common good ended up with a situation where everyone looked out only for himself because he could count on no one else.

One aspect of the Great Terror was the 'cult' of Stalin, as it subsequently came to be called. In fact, it was Stalin's deification: he was omnipotent, omnipresent, omniscient, infallible, and he remained such until his death in 1953. When he criticized a new opera, the composer groveled. When he pronounced on linguistics, philologists fell silent. At party congresses, deputies vied with each other, extolling the greatness of the 'leader,' while he sat modestly on the side, taking in his praises. Osip Mandelshtam, widely considered one of the century's great Russian poets, paid with his life for a poem about the dictator that contained the following lines:

His fingers are fat as grubs
And the words, final as lead weights, fall from his lips,
His cockroach whiskers leer
And his boot tops gleam.
Around him a rabble of thin-necked leaders –

Fawning half men for him to play with.

They whinny, purr or whine,

As he prates and points a finger,

One by one forging his laws, to be flung

Like horseshoes at the head, the eye or the groin.

And every killing is a treat.[23]

One possible explanation of the deification of leaders common to most Communist regimes is that inasmuch as omnipotence and omniscience are universal qualities of divinities, it is natural to attribute to individuals endowed with them divine qualities.

His veneration caused Stalin progressively to lose touch with reality. Surrounded by sycophants, he had no knowledge of the true condition of his realm. Afraid of assassination, he never traveled in the country, and formed an image of its life from specially prepared films, in which, according to his lieutenant and eventual successor Nikita Khrushchev, collective-farm workers sat at tables 'bending from the weight of turkeys and geese.'

The one institution familiar with Soviet reality was the security police, successively called the Cheka (1917–22), the GPU and OGPU (1922–34), the NKVD (1934–54), and the KGB (1954–91). It was the principal organ of terror, enjoying wide latitude in disposing of all enemies of the regime, real, potential, or suspected. It also operated the vast empire of forced-labor camps. Having abolished all outlets of public opinion, the government relied on the security police to inform it of the public mood, which it did through a vast network of agents and informants. In many respects, in Stalin's waning years the security organs usurped the powers that Lenin had bestowed on the Communist Party.

Stalin was the first Communist to realize and exploit the political potential of Russian nationalism. Marxism viewed nationalism in all its manifestations as a device that the bourgeoisie manipulated to deflect the masses from their true mission, the class struggle. Lenin himself was a stranger to patriotic sentiments. He rather felt contempt for his own people, to whom he would refer in confidential communications using such unflattering terms as 'Soviet bunglers and slobs.' He once told the writer Maxim Gorky that 'an intelligent Russian is almost always a Jew or someone with Jewish blood in his veins.'[24]

Not so Stalin. Close contact with the cadres convinced him that nationalism and xenophobia found a much readier response in the country than the nebulous ideals of international Communism. Accordingly, he began, cautiously at first and then with increasing boldness, to identify himself with Russian chauvinism, deliberately disassociating the Soviet regime from the notion, widespread at the time in Russia and abroad, that Communism served the interests of a worldwide Jewish conspiracy. A rabid anti-Semite, he systematically dismissed Jews from government positions. During his alliance with Hitler, he promised von Ribbentrop, Hitler's foreign minister, that as soon as he found suitable Gentile replacements, he would remove all Jews from leading posts.[25] Shortly before his death, he planned the deportation of the entire Soviet Jewish population to Siberia.

In 1934, after Hitler's ascent to power, Stalin ordered a complete reversal of the party line on Russian patriotism. Love of fatherland, previously condemned, was henceforth actively promoted, and the teaching of history, which in good Marxist fashion had until then concentrated on class struggles, began to stress Russia's achievements in war and peace. By the time Stalin died, Soviet Communism had dissolved in Russian nationalism: such prestige as the regime enjoyed was due to its victory in World War II and its subsequent success, thanks to pioneering work in intercontinental missiles and space programs, in elevating Russia to the status of a great world power, an equal of the United States. To this day, whatever nostalgia Russians feel for the Soviet Union derives not from longing for its domestic regime – i.e., Communism – but almost exclusively from the remembrance of how heady it was to be respected and feared by other nations.

At this point it is appropriate to inquire whether the twenty-five-year dictatorship of Stalin was a natural, that is, inevitable, consequence of the regime established by Lenin or an accident that allowed a psychopath to hijack the revolution. There is no doubt that Stalin displayed symptoms of clinical paranoia, megalomania, and sadism; this was later confirmed by some of his closest associates. Yet it must be borne in mind that he had succeeded Lenin not by a coup d'état but step by step, promoted by the party itself. He was its choice. Historians who maintain that Lenin's mantle should have fallen either on Trotsky or Bukharin ignore the fact that though he admired both these men, Lenin did not consider them suitable successors. The despotic powers that Stalin exercised were put in place by Lenin. It was Lenin who introduced mass terror with hostage taking and concentration camps, who viewed law and courts as 'substantiating and legitimizing' terror, who authorized Articles 57 and 58 of the Criminal Code, omnibus clauses that Stalin used to execute and imprison millions of innocent citizens. And it was Lenin who had the party pass a resolution outlawing 'factions,' which enabled Stalin to dispose of anyone who disagreed with him as a 'deviationist.' Personal dictatorship was inherent in the system that Lenin created, even though he himself preferred to operate in a more collegial manner. From 'The party is always right' it was an easy transition to 'The leader of the party is always right.' And once this principle was accepted, how the autocratic leadership would be exercised was a matter of chance.

Vyacheslav Molotov served both Lenin and Stalin in highly confidential posts longer than any other Bolshevik. When asked in his old age who of the two was the more 'severe,' he replied without hesitation, 'Lenin, of course...I recall how he scolded Stalin for softness and liberalism.'[26] Which should dispose of the myth, popularized first by Trotsky and then by Khrushchev, that Stalinism meant a repudiation of Leninism.

World War II was initiated by Germany, bent on avenging its defeat of 1918 and subjugating Europe. But the Soviet Union, for its own reasons, aided and abetted Hitler's aggressive designs and hence bore much responsibility for this most terrible of all wars.

The failure of every attempt to incite revolution in Europe, culminating in the disastrous Polish campaign, persuaded the Soviet leadership that the best hope for spreading their regime was to promote another world war. In January 1925, Stalin said, 'Struggles, conflicts and wars among our enemies are... our greatest ally.' They are 'without a doubt, the greatest support of our government and our revolution.' Referring to the inevitability of another global conflict, he added ominously, 'If war does break out, we will not sit with folded arms – we will have to take the field, but we will be the *last* to do so. And we shall do so in order to throw the decisive load on the scale.'[27]

In line with this reasoning, from the early 1920s until 1933, the Soviet Union engaged in secret collaboration with the German military to enable it to circumvent the provisions of the Versailles Treaty, which prohibited or severely limited Germany's manufacture of tanks, aircraft, submarines, and poison gas. Moscow allowed the Germans to produce and test these weapons on its territory, while the Germans, reciprocating, invited Red Army officers to attend its general-staff courses, which prepared the strategy and tactics of the blitzkrieg. (The Soviet Union also actively collaborated with Fascist Italy in the naval field.)

Such considerations, too, explain why in 1932–33 Stalin helped Hitler come to power, by forbidding German Communists to make common cause with the Social Democrats against the Nazis in parliamentary elections. (See chapter 4.) The German Social Democrats were pro-Western. The Nazis, Stalin reasoned, although vehemently anti-Communist, would direct their aggression against the Western democracies and leave the Soviet Union alone. Such thinking lay behind his decision in August 1939 to sign a nonaggression treaty with Berlin that included a secret protocol dividing Poland between

Russia and Germany. He clearly counted on a repetition of the 1914–18 war of attrition, which would leave the 'capitalist' belligerents so exhausted that the USSR could sweep into Europe virtually unopposed. After Germany and Russia had divided Poland, Molotov, Stalin's closest confidant and the man who, as foreign minister, had signed the nonaggression treaty, delivered a speech in which, assailing France and England for waging war on Hitler, he declared that 'the ideology of Hitlerism, as any ideological system, can be accepted or rejected: this is a matter of political opinion.' Communist parties everywhere were instructed to depict Britain and France as reactionary and aggressive. The entire policy proved to be a gigantic miscalculation.

When, in 1940, Hitler's forces crushed the Allied armies in France and then proceeded to occupy most of the continent, Stalin entered into a virtual alliance with Nazi Germany, furnishing it foodstuffs, metals, and other scarce matériel. He even turned over to Hitler some German Communists who had sought refuge in the USSR. It seemed so plausible that Hitler would continue the profitable collaboration with Moscow that Stalin ignored warnings from both Allied and his own intelligence services that the Germans were massing troops in Poland for an assault on the Soviet Union.

The Red Army, stripped by the purges of its most experienced officers and forbidden to prepare for the onslaught, suffered in the initial months of the war mind-boggling losses in men and equipment, with millions of Red Army troops taken prisoner.

Once Stalin had recovered from the shock, he took charge of the defenses. The pretense that the country was fighting for

Communism was quickly abandoned: invoking religion and the military glories of the tsarist era, the nation was exhorted to fight for 'Holy Russia.' Resistance, which at first appeared hopeless, was abetted by Hitler's strategic blunders and by the barbaric warfare the invaders waged. To avoid Napoleon's mistake in advancing on Moscow, Hitler sent large forces north, against Leningrad, and south, against Kiev. In these operations, the Wehrmacht captured still more prisoners but lost valuable time, and when it finally resumed the offensive against the capital, winter had set in and the attack bogged down. Russians and Ukrainians, not a few of whom had at first welcomed the Germans, soon realized that the Nazis had come not to liberate them from the Communists but to impose on them even worse slavery. They showed tremendous courage and tenacity in fighting an enemy vastly superior in equipment. The war on the eastern front eventually broke the back of the German army and determined the outcome of World War II. It was bought at a terrible price. The Red command treated soldiers as expendable material, throwing them into battle without regard for casualties. It was not uncommon for major battles to inflict on the Red Army hundreds of thousands of fatalities. In the defense of Kiev in the summer of 1941, it lost 616,000 lives; in the Donbass offensive two years later, 661,000. Foreign scholars estimate total Soviet war losses at 20 million fatalities, 8.7 million of them in combat.[28] These combat losses were more than three times those suffered by the Wehrmacht on the eastern front (2.6 million). Around 5 million Soviet troops were taken prisoner, of whom anywhere between 1.9 and 3.6 million perished in German captivity from malnutrition, shooting, or gassing.

Stalin's reward for victory was territorial expansion. Soviet troops occupied and installed Communist regimes in most of eastern and central Europe, with a combined population of some 90 million and a territory exceeding that of France and West Germany combined. Yugoslavia and Albania also went Communist.

Even more impressive was the fact that the Chinese Communists, with whom Moscow had had, for a quarter of a century, a love-hate relationship, won the civil war against the U.S.-backed armies of the Kuomintang and by 1949 gained control of all China. The spread of Communism to the rest of the world seemed only a matter of time.

World War II was the only event in the history of the Soviet Union that brought the nation and the government closer together: 'After the German attack in June 1941, for the first time in Soviet history official claims coincided with the truth: the Germans *were* brutal invaders, the nation was *genuinely* faced with a struggle for survival.'[29] The war provided the Communist regime, as defender of the people, with a legitimacy that until then it had lacked. But the widely held hope that as a result of this collaboration Stalin would relax his rule and grant his people more freedom did not materialize. In the few years left to him, he showed no sign of mellowing.

The death of Stalin confronted his successors with a quandary. They felt they had to repudiate the demented dictator and his murderous policies, and yet they needed to preserve the system that he had managed for nearly thirty years because their power and privilege derived from it. They solved the problem by reconnecting Communism to Lenin. In 1956, in a secret speech to the Twentieth Party Congress, the first to convene since Stalin's death, Nikita Khrushchev, the new first secretary, revealed some of the crimes that Stalin had perpetrated against the Communist *nomenklatura*. As a result of these revelations, Stalin promptly turned into a nonperson: his corpse was removed from the mausoleum that he had shared with Lenin, Stalingrad was renamed Volgograd, and with the efficiency of which the Soviet bureaucracy was justly proud, his countless portraits, statues, and place-names vanished. It was as if the three decades of Stalin's rule were a grand error, though no attempt was made to explain such a 'mistake.' For there were only two possible solutions, neither acceptable: either Marx's materialist theory was wrong and history was, after all, determined by politics and politicians, or else the Soviet Union was not a Marxist state.

The anti-Stalin campaign was a bold and perhaps even necessary move, but its effect was to undermine the legitimacy of this regime that had permitted such massive crimes: Khrushchev's revelations initiated the slow but inexorable delegitimization of Communism.

To compensate for de-Stalinization and infuse new life into the system, Khrushchev initiated the deification of Lenin with such intensity that it would outlive the collapse of the Soviet Union. Asked in 1999 to name the ten greatest men in all history, Russians listed Peter I first and Lenin third, after Pushkin. (In spite of Khrushchev's efforts, Stalin rated fourth.)

Freed from the Stalinist terror, the *nomenklatura* set itself to enjoy the kind of life to which it felt entitled by virtue of its responsibilities and exalted status. It emancipated itself from the control of the party's leading organs with surprising speed.

Khrushchev relaxed somewhat the dead dictator's regime without changing its basic institutions or laws: one-party rule remained in place, as did the ubiquitous secret police and censorship. Nevertheless, life for Soviet citizens eased considerably. Millions of concentration-camp inmates regained their freedom. Many victims of repression were rehabilitated, which did not benefit them but brought relief to their families. Limited contacts with foreign nationals were permitted once again. More visitors from abroad received entry visas, and more Soviet citizens could travel outside the USSR. The jamming of foreign short-wave broadcasts continued as before, but it was not foolproof, so that the Soviet public could obtain a more realistic picture of life abroad as well as at home.

The effect was to open people's eyes. In the 1970s Mikhail Gorbachev was already high up in the Communist hierarchy when he visited Italy, France, Belgium, and West Germany. He was stunned by what he saw – not merely by the West's living standards but by its civil culture. As a result, his 'previous belief in the superiority of socialist democracy over the bourgeois system was shaken': 'We were amazed by the open and relaxed attitude of the people we met,' he would recall in his memoirs, 'and marvelled at their unrestrained judgment of everything, including the activity of their governments and their national and local politicians.' His future rival, Boris Yeltsin, the first elected head of state of sovereign Russia, was similarly affected by a trip to the United States in 1989. The journey was for him an 'endless row of collapsed stereotypes and clichés.' Having inspected a supermarket in Houston, he wondered aloud: 'What have they done to our poor people?' The experience, his companion thought, had destroyed in Yeltsin whatever still remained of his Communist faith. It turned out that Stalin had been right: the system could survive only if it kept its people, including the highest officials, fully insulated from the external world.

As regards foreign policy, Stalin's heirs reevaluated and abandoned his confrontational strategy, concluding that capitalism, after all, did not teeter on the brink of collapse: sixty years after the predictions of Eduard Bernstein, the Politburo adopted his thesis that socialism would triumph not by revolution, let alone by war, but by nonviolent means. The new slogan was 'peaceful coexistence.' Foreign Communists were instructed to enter into coalitions not only with the Third World national bourgeoisie but also with the socialists, whom Lenin had viewed as Communism's worst enemy.

Meanwhile, the post-Stalinist regime concentrated on two tasks: military buildup and penetration into the Third World.

Although it continued to maintain an awesome conventional force, the new leadership decided that the decisive weapons of the future would be nuclear missiles. This conclusion was partly forced on it by the need to reduce the military budget, the bulk of which went to pay for conventional forces. But it also had a theoretical basis. Moscow rejected the Western view that nuclear weapons served only one purpose, namely deterrence, and made a major effort to develop rockets capable of engaging in offensive operations across continents. The effort culminated in October 1957 in the successful launching of *Sputnik*, the world's first artificial satellite, which demonstrated Soviet progress in missile technology that potentially threatened the continental United States. For the next thirty years, the Soviet government poured immense sums into the military budget – by recent estimates, as much as 25 to 30 and perhaps even 40 percent of its national income. Its military prowess, especially in nuclear weaponry and the space program, gained the Soviet Union international recognition as a 'superpower.' This status was illusory, since it rested entirely on the regime's ability to blackmail foreign powers with its nuclear arsenal, the resort to which risked total destruction of the Soviet Union; furthermore it severely drained the nation's economic resources, contributing ultimately to its downfall.

The policy of active engagement in the Third World had as one of its objectives outflanking the West and striking at its one-time colonial dependencies, with which the West continued to maintain close economic relations. But expansion also boosted domestic morale: the prospect of Communist and pro-Communist regimes spreading relentlessly outward from their Soviet core created another illusion, namely that Communism's advance was unstoppable. Its corollary effect was to make all resistance to Communism at home appear futile. But expansion was a costly ploy, since gaining support of Third World countries required massive subsidies in the form of grants and loans that would never be repaid. It proved a dubious investment as well for, as we shall note later, the allies won in this manner turned out to be unreliable.

In 1964, his colleagues deposed Khrushchev: the establishment had grown weary of his restless activity and yearned, in the words of his son, 'for calm and stability.' His place was taken by Leonid Brezhnev, who would serve as first secretary for eighteen years, even though late in life he showed distinct signs of senility: the machine simply ground on.

Year by year, the Soviet regime decayed. The economy stagnated, falling ever more behind those of the advanced industrial countries. With fear of draconian punishment gone, workers had little incentive to exert themselves: as they cynically explained, 'They pretend to pay us and we pretend to work.' Workers who showed zeal risked being accused by their colleagues of 'provocation' and roughed up. The central planning apparatus concentrated on doing what it knew best: turning out the same goods and in the process missing out on such innovations as plastics, synthetic fibers, and, above all, computers. Insistence on tight control of information meant that the USSR did not participate in advances in information technology, which revolutionized Western economies. The living standards of ordinary citizens, though better than in Stalin's day, fell below even the low minimal norms set by the state: thus in the late 1980s, nearly one-half of the Soviet population earned less than ten dollars a month. Drunkenness was endemic: the Soviet Union could boast the highest rate of alcohol consumption in the world, as well as the highest rate of alcoholic deaths. Nothing illustrated better the ebbing vitality of its citizens than demographic statistics: the population, which under tsarism had grown at the most rapid rate in Europe, by the 1970s showed a deficit, as more Russians (and Ukrainians) died each year than were born.

Corruption flourished: to get anything done, one had to bribe officials in charge of goods and services. High posts were sold to the highest bidders. Figures available for the

Azerbaijani republic reveal regular tariffs charged for all executive offices, including those in the party; the highest prices were fetched by those posts that offered the greatest opportunities for bribe taking and theft of public property. Russians became so accustomed to corruption they were quite prepared to bribe without ensuring that it served its purpose. For example:

On a Moscow market there stood a stall selling all kinds of odds and ends operated by an invalid. This man was prepared for a certain price to obtain any young person desirous of enrolling at the university admission to any faculty....[Because of the difficulties of getting into the university] this disabled veteran, who disposed of magic powers and abilities to procure admission, enjoyed an enormous business from doting parents who, trembling with eagerness, pressed into his hands the requested sum. The disabled veteran followed the most scrupulous business principles and always warned his clients that he was not omnipotent, that, naturally, he would do all in his power but could not guarantee success: in case their daughter or son failed to gain admission, he promised to refund the money. And indeed, whenever he did fail, the parents received their money back. But he was often successful, succeeding time and again, and in this manner secured a wide clientele willing to pay.

And what did he do for it? Nothing! He did nothing at all, sought out no one and spoke to no one; he had no contacts with any faculty or school administrators. But he earned well, proceeding on the following premise: If the parents were so eager for their child to study, they would not rely exclusively on his support but explore also other channels, possibly seeking to acquire, with an appropriate gift, another helper, one high up. And one of these pulleys would grab – which one, they would never find out. Secondly, it was quite conceivable that the youth would be seized with such ambition that he would prepare thoroughly for the [entrance] examination and, despite all difficulties, clear the hurdle. And if all went amiss, he would refund the money.[30]

No moral onus was attached to stealing state property. Indeed, a popular saying encouraged it by telling Soviet citizens, 'If you don't steal from the government, you are stealing from your family.' This manner of thinking led to the corruption of the entire nation.

The general relaxation encouraged bolder spirits to challenge the regime, giving rise to the phenomenon of dissidence. The dissidents were punished in the customary manner, to which Brezhnev's security chief, Iurii Andropov, added the innovation of confining them to mental institutions, where they were subjected to drug treatments and other tortures. It is estimated that by the late 1980s, the KGB had a staff of at least 480,000, of whom about a quarter of a million, assisted by tens of millions of informants, engaged in domestic counterintelligence and surveillance.[31] But the movement once started would not stop, and even if their numbers were minuscule, dissidents continued to sap the government's prestige.

So did developments among Soviet dependencies in Eastern Europe. In 1956, when the Hungarians rebelled to reclaim their national independence, Moscow crushed their defiance with military force. The same happened in 1968 when the Czech Communists attempted to adopt democratic socialism. But when in Poland in the 1970s there emerged a powerful trade union movement called Solidarity, which challenged the Communist regime head-on, Moscow could no longer muster the courage to intervene. Afraid lest the movement infect Soviet workers, it insisted that the Polish Communists take the initiative in crushing Solidarity. After long hesitation, in December 1981, the Polish government imposed martial law on the country and arrested nearly all the leaders of the labor movement.

In the mid-1980s, the Soviet Union confronted a genuine crisis, not one artificially concocted to justify the dictatorship. It was caused by a progressive atrophy of all sectors of public life. It confronted the Communist regime for the first time with a problem that could not be solved by force. It required far-reaching reform – that is, concessions.

Resolution was postponed for a while by the choice of elderly and sometimes sick first secretaries, who made certain not to rock the boat. But by 1985 the decision could no longer be put off. The Communist bloc found itself in what Lenin had defined as a 'revolutionary situation': the bloc's governments could no longer rule in the accustomed manner, and the people would no longer allow themselves to be thus ruled. The result was a tense stalemate that could explode in revolution. To avert the danger, in 1985 the Politburo appointed a relatively young member, Mikhail Gorbachev, as its first secretary. His task was to reanimate the system without upsetting its foundations. This assignment proved impossible to accomplish because all efforts at reform ran into the resistance of the entrenched *nomenklatura*, which quietly sabotaged them. By 1988, Gorbachev and his advisers had concluded that

Communism was unreformable and took steps to transform the USSR into a democratic socialist state.

First came glasnost, which meant an end to government secrecy and a significant relaxation of censorship. The regime confronted a dilemma: it could either continue stifling all opinion and slowly suffocate the country or it could release it and risk a destructive explosion. Gorbachev chose what he hoped would be a controlled explosion. This proved an extremely dangerous step. Andropov, the long-term head of the KGB and Brezhnev's immediate successor, had warned that relaxing controls on speech could bring down the whole regime:

> Too many groups have suffered under the repression in our country....If we open up all the valves at once, and people start to express their grievances, there will be an avalanche and we will have no means of stopping it.[32]

The accumulated grievances, now given outlets, did indeed erupt in the open, sweeping away the official myths and the entire surreality resting on them.

Gorbachev did not stop at glasnost; he ended the political monopoly of the Communist Party by authorizing the con-vocation of a Congress of People's Deputies, a number of whose representatives were to be directly chosen by the citizens. For the first time since 1917, the nation was given a voice in the election of its officials. It chose many non-Communists and even anti-Communists, among them Boris Yeltsin, the unorthodox head of the Moscow Party organization who had gained great popularity by assailing the *nomenklatura*'s privileges. From then on, events moved at a dizzying speed. In 1989, the Berlin Wall, the symbol of the impassable separation between East and West, came down, because Moscow had refused to send military forces to help the East German government reassert its authority. One satellite country after another declared its independence from Moscow. Ineffective efforts were made to prevent the Soviet republics from following suit. In December 1991, after an abortive putsch of die-hard Communists bent on stopping the further disintegration of the USSR, Yeltsin, who earlier in the year had been elected president of the Russian republic, declared Russia a sovereign state, thereby dissolving the Soviet Union. One of his first acts was to outlaw the Communist Party. The new government proclaimed democracy and the free market. The *nomenklatura*, which had the power to reverse the progress of events, was bought off by being allowed to appropriate a great deal of state property.

The speed with which these events unfolded revealed the extreme fragility of an empire that had seemed indestructible; its dissolution resembled that of the tsarist empire three-quarters of a century earlier. In both cases, the rigidity of the regime and its lack of close contact with the population left it, in its hour of desperate need, friendless and abandoned.

Communism in Russia simply burned itself out. It had demanded too much and delivered too little, creating an atmosphere of apathy in which the only pleasures were little ones and the future held no prospects. By the 1980s even the Soviet elite had lost faith in Communism, as it watched the outside world overtake the country in every field of endeavor except military expenditures and alcohol consumption. Its self-confidence gone, it put up feeble resistance and, seizing for its own benefit a great deal of state property, accepted the regime's demise with equanimity.

IV   *Reception in the West*

Initially, the outbreak of the March 1917 revolution in Russia aroused little interest in western Europe: the leading Swiss daily, *Neue Zürcher Zeitung*, from which Lenin first learned of the turmoil in his homeland, carried the information on page 2, as a routine news item. Engrossed in a ferocious war, Europe had little time to spare for happenings in distant Russia, which, after its defeats in 1915, had for all practical purposes ceased to count as a belligerent. What reaction there was tended to be positive, due to the belief that the Provisional Government, which at first enjoyed near universal support, would reengage in the war. The United States, ever ready to welcome new members into the community of democratic nations, was the first to extend diplomatic recognition to the new government.

This positive attitude did not change immediately after the Bolsheviks had toppled the Provisional Government. Aware of Lenin's links with Imperial Germany, the Allied powers viewed him and his regime with misgivings, but so eager were they to reactivate the eastern front that they were prepared to court any Russian government, even the Bolsheviks. The courting ended in March 1918, following the conclusion of the Brest-Litovsk treaty, which took Soviet Russia out of the war. The Allies now shifted their support to the White armies

forming in southern Russia and Siberia because they committed themselves to toppling the pro-German Bolsheviks and
resuming combat operations against the Central Powers. The
support involved mostly supplies. Small Allied contingents
landed, with Lenin's consent, in the northern Russian ports of
Murmansk and Arkhangelsk to keep them from falling into
German hands. American troops deployed in eastern Siberia;
their main contribution was to keep that vast region out of
Japanese hands. Except for occasional skirmishing, neither the
British nor the Americans engaged in combat. The myth of
massive capitalist intervention in the Russian civil war
was concocted later by Stalin as part of an anti-Western
campaign.

The termination of hostilities in November 1918 deprived
the Allied involvement in Russia of any justification. If the
British nevertheless continued to help the White side in the
civil war, they did so largely on the insistence of Winston
Churchill, then the First Lord of the Admiralty, who recog-
nized, as did few others, the danger that Communism posed to
the world – just as in the 1930s he would anticipate the Nazi
threat. He entertained the fantastic notion of an international
crusade to dislodge the Communists from power. War-weary
Europe paid no heed to such proposals. But David Lloyd
George, Britain's Liberal prime minister, in need of Tory
support, humored Churchill even though personally he was
prepared to come to terms with Lenin, whom he believed to be
a lesser threat to British interests than a revived tsarism. But
by the end of 1919, after the White armies had been all but
crushed, Lloyd George had had enough and ordered British
support withdrawn from the Whites. Churchill, even as he

yielded, warned of dire consequences from a future coalition of Germany, Soviet Russia, and Japan:

> If we abandon Russia, Germany and Japan will not. The new states which it is hoped to bring into being in the East of Europe will be crushed between Russian Bolshevism and Germany....In five years, or even less, it will be apparent that the whole fruits of our victories have been lost.

In 1921, Britain, which set the pace in these matters, opened commercial negotiations with Soviet Russia; diplomatic recognition came soon afterward. The rest of Europe followed suit. Alone of the great powers, the United States refused to recognize a government that had, as its stated objective, the destruction of the international state system; it did so only in 1933.

The Soviet government conducted foreign relations on two distinct levels: the diplomatic and the subversive. In the 1920s, Soviet 'political representatives' took over embassies of the tsarist government in the capitals of 'bourgeois' states, from where they conducted their work with the same decorum as diplomats of any other country. But the real action took place out of sight: here operated agents of the Communist International charged with overthrowing the very governments to which Soviet envoys were accredited. Whenever foreign states lodged protests against these subversive activities, Moscow, with as straight a face as it could muster, responded that the Communist parties as well as the International were private organizations, for the activities of which it bore no responsibility.

If the Allies had supported anti-Communist forces in Russia without much conviction, halfheartedly and stingily, Moscow backed antidemocratic forces in the West with all the resources at its disposal.

The Third International, or Comintern, which Trotsky called the 'General Staff of the World Revolution,' was founded in Moscow in March 1919, but it took shape only a year later, in the summer of 1920, by which time the civil war was virtually over and the Communists could concentrate on foreign affairs. The mood was heady: the Red Army, encountering virtually no resistance, was advancing on Warsaw, and there seemed nothing to stop it from marching into Germany and England, both of which, Lenin believed, were ripe for revolution. The resolutions of the Comintern's Second Congress (1920) opened with the claim that 'decisive struggles confront the world proletariat. The epoch in which we are now living is the epoch of open civil wars. The decisive hour is approaching.'[1] In a secret communication to Stalin, who at the time was at the Polish front, Lenin wrote:

> The situation in the Comintern splendid. Zinoviev, Bukharin, and I, too, think that revolution in Italy should be exacerbated immediately. My personal opinion is that to this end, Hungary should be sovietized, and perhaps also Czechia and Romania. We have to think it over carefully. Communicate your detailed conclusion. German Communists think that Germany is capable of mustering three hundred thousand troops from the *lumpen* against us.[2]*

The last sentence of this message demonstrates that Moscow intended the Red Army to proceed from conquered Poland into Germany and there help its sympathizers seize power.

---

* *Lumpenproletariat*, or 'scamp proletarians,' were in socialist language marginal laborers willing to sell themselves to the 'bourgeoisie.'

As events were to show, Lenin completely misread the situation in Europe. The experience of October and November 1917, when he had to overcome the hesitations of his lieutenants to launch a successful coup d'état, persuaded him that caution was cowardice; so great was his prestige by now that he carried along even the most skeptical among them.

Present at the 1920 congress of the Comintern were revolutionaries from many countries of Europe and overseas, prepared to break with moderate socialists and follow the leadership of the Russian Bolsheviks, the only Marxists who had succeeded in founding a socialist state. Lenin made it no secret that he envisaged the Comintern as a branch of the Russian Communist Party, organized on its model and subject to its orders. The 1920 congress demanded of its associates that they impose on their members 'iron military discipline' and show 'the fullest comradely confidence' in the center, i.e., Moscow. Their immediate mission was to infiltrate and take over all mass organizations in their respective countries. To pursue this objective in the trade unions, in Lenin's words, Communists must 'in case of necessity...resort to every kind of trick, cunning, illegal expedient, concealment, suppression of truth.'[3] The ultimate goal of member parties was to assist the Comintern in waging 'armed insurrection' against existing bourgeois governments and replacing them with Communist regimes. These would ultimately fuse into a worldwide Soviet Socialist Republic.

The Congress adopted, with token dissent, a twenty-one-point list of prerequisites for admission to the Comintern. The most important were the following:

2. All organizations aspiring to membership are to expel from their ranks 'reformists and centrists';

3. Communists are to create in practically every European and American country a 'parallel illegal organization,' which, at the decisive moment, will surface and take charge of the revolution;

14. 'Every party which wishes to join the Communist International is obligated to give unconditional support to any Soviet republic in its struggle against counter-revolutionary forces';

21. 'Those members of the party who reject in principle the conditions and theses put forward by the Communist International are to be expelled from the party.'[4]

Since everything that Moscow disapproved of was, by definition, 'counterrevolutionary,' Article 14 established the principle that for Communists of all nationalities the interests and wishes of the Soviet Union were supreme, superseding those of their own countries.

Driven by Lenin's customary energy, the Comintern managed, throughout Europe, to split socialist movements and create Communist parties, which it both directed and secretly financed. To this extent, it succeeded. But in terms of its ultimate objectives, the Comintern proved a dismal failure. For one, its assumption that the capitalist countries stood on the brink of civil war turned out to be entirely false, for no such war broke out in any Western country; and wherever it threatened, it was quickly crushed. Secondly, although the Communists won a considerable following in powerful labor unions in several countries, especially those with predominantly

Catholic populations (Spain, Italy, and France), they nowhere gained parliamentary majorities. As a consequence, even where they managed to acquire a sizable following, the Communist parties turned into a permanent opposition – isolated and therefore impotent. Working under strict orders from Moscow to regard the Social Democrats as the principal enemy, they weakened the socialist as well as Communist movements and in some countries paved the way for right-wing dictatorships, of which they were the first victims.

This emerged most clearly in Weimar Germany. Here in the late 1920s a furious conflict pitted three powerful parties against one another: the Social Democrats, Communists, and Nazis. In this clash, Moscow consistently favored the Nazis over the Social Democrats, whom it called 'social Fascists' and continued to regard as its principal enemy. In line with this reasoning, it forbade the German Communists to collaborate with the Social Democrats. In the critical November 1932 elections to the Reichstag (parliament), the Social Democrats won over 7 million votes and the Communists 6 million: their combined vote exceeded the Nazi vote by 1.5 million. In terms of parliamentary seats, they gained between them 221, against the Nazi 196. Had they joined forces, the two left-wing parties would have defeated Hitler at the polls and prevented him from assuming the chancellorship. It thus was the tacit alliance between the Communists and the National Socialists that destroyed democracy in Germany and brought Hitler to power.

In the 1930s, when the Soviet Union was undergoing its most traumatic experiences – collectivization, famine, and the Great

Terror – its image in the West greatly improved because of two events that deeply affected the West's self-confidence: the Depression and the rise of Nazism. The massive unemployment that struck the industrial democracies seemed to confirm Marx's prediction that capitalism was condemned to undergo crises of mounting severity until it finally collapsed. The contrast between Communist Russia forging ahead with her grandiose program of economic construction that assured full employment and the idleness of Western industries convinced many liberal observers that capitalism was indeed doomed. Communism also gained a following by advocating abroad policies that it proscribed and heavily punished in its own domain, such as the right of labor to organize and the demands of minorities (e.g., American blacks) to equality. Soviet support of the anti-Fascist cause in the Spanish civil war had the same effect.

Most European Communists and sympathizers were not oblivious to the odious aspects of Communist rule, but they rationalized them in various ways: by blaming extraneous causes, such as the legacy of tsarism and the hostility of the 'capitalist' West, or by viewing them as unavoidable by-products of an unprecedented effort to build a completely new society. The writer Arthur Koestler, who joined the German Communist Party in 1932 and lived for a year in the Soviet Union (he broke with the movement in 1938), explained as follows the mental processes that enabled both party members and sympathizers to overlook the terror and starvation the Soviet regime inflicted on its people:

> I learned to classify automatically everything that shocked me

as the 'heritage of the past' and everything I liked as 'seeds of the future.' By setting up this automatic sorting machine in his mind, it was still possible in 1932 for a European to live in Russia and yet to remain a Communist.[5]

Koestler compared joining the Communist Party to a spiritual conversion:

To say that one had 'seen the light' is a poor description of the mental rapture which only the convert knows.... The new light seems to pour from all directions across the skull; the whole universe falls into a pattern like the stray pieces of a jigsaw puzzle assembled by magic at one stroke. There is now an answer to every question, doubts and conflicts are a matter of the tortured past.... Nothing henceforth can disturb the convert's inner peace and serenity – except the occasional fear of losing faith again, losing thereby what alone makes life worth living, and falling back into the outer darkness.[6]

In northern Europe and the United States, where neither socialism nor Communism had much of a following, Moscow won useful allies among liberals and 'fellow travelers,' mostly intellectuals who, without joining the party, promoted its objectives. They were of the greatest importance to it because, unlike party members, who were suspected of speaking at the party's command, they expressed personal convictions. The mind-set of the fellow traveler is exemplified by the American journalist Lincoln Steffens, who in 1919 coined a celebrated and oft-quoted epigram about Soviet Russia: 'I have seen the future, and it works.' It turns out that he penned these words on a train crossing Sweden on the way to Moscow, before having set foot on Soviet soil. Later, while vacationing at Karlsbad, an elegant Czech spa, he wrote a friend: 'I am patriot for Russia, the Future is there. Russia will win out and it will save the world. That is my belief. But I don't want to live there.'

Classic fellow travelers were Sidney and Beatrice Webb, two respected English socialists whose political and scholarly career went back to the Fabian Society. The Webbs had initially been hostile to the Bolshevik regime, but in 1932 they radically changed their minds. They went on a three-week journey to the USSR, where they received royal treatment. They were enchanted by everything they saw and, in their own words, 'fell in love with Russia.' In 1935, working from printed materials supplied to them by their hosts, they published a two-volume treatise, *Soviet Communism, a New Civilisation?* (In the 1941 edition the question mark was dropped.) Treating Soviet documentation as they would official British sources, and having each page 'checked for errors' by the Soviet embassy, they provided a fictional account of Soviet life without the slightest awareness of the propagandistic purpose of the literature from which they drew their information. Suffice it to say that they denied, on the basis of Soviet writings, that Stalin was a dictator; indeed, they maintained, he ruled collegially and, in their view, enjoyed less power than the president of the United States or the British prime minister. Police terror, famines, and censorship they either ignored, minimized, or depicted as comparable to practices in the capitalist world. Even so, fellow Fabian George Bernard Shaw praised their turgid and uncritical treatise of nearly 1,200 pages as 'the first really scientific analysis of the Soviet State.'

In 1942, Beatrice Webb published a shorter book on the subject, *The Truth About Soviet Russia*, in which, with reference to the 1936 Soviet 'constitution,' she described the USSR as 'the most inclusive and equalized democracy in the world.'

The Webbs were too intelligent and too familiar with scholarly methods not to realize how one-sided were their views of Soviet Communism. If they nevertheless failed to provide a more balanced picture, the reason must be sought in a desperate psychological need – at a time when Western civilization seemed to be facing final collapse – for a perfect world. To depict it, they set up in their minds the kind of 'sorting machine' alluded to by Koestler, which enabled them automatically to eject all adverse information.

Not all Western intellectuals were taken in, of course. Interestingly, the ones who best saw through the Communist facade were not scientists -- natural or social – but humanists: novelists, poets, and philosophers. Instead of being captivated by abstractions and then interpreting reality in their light, they saw reality on its own terms.

Bertrand Russell, a leading English philosopher, visited Soviet Russia in 1920 as a member of the British Labour Delegation. He approached the Soviet experiment with sympathy: capitalism, in his judgment, was doomed, whereas 'Communism is necessary to the world....Bolshevism deserves the gratitude and admiration of all the progressive part of mankind.' This he wrote on his return, in *The Practice and Theory of Bolshevism*. But such sentiments were the 'theory.' The 'practice,' which he observed with a keen eye, left him skeptical: he remarked with dismay on the quasi-religious fanaticism of the Bolsheviks, their impatience, and their dogmatism. And he doubted whether it was possible to construct Communism in a country as poor as Russia, the majority of whose population was hostile to it.

The French novelist André Gide, similarly declaring his 'admiration' and 'love' for the Soviet Union, began as another classic fellow traveler. The USSR was to him 'more than a chosen land'; it was utopia 'in the process of becoming reality.' He paid it a visit in the summer of 1936, while the sham 'trial' of Zinoviev and Kamenev was under way. Back in France, he published a slender volume, *Return from the U.S.S.R.* In this confused account of his visit, in which praise and disapproval contend without arriving at a clear verdict, Gide justified his right to criticize the Soviet experiment 'precisely because of his admiration.' While in Russia, he wrote, he shed 'tears of overflowing joy, of tenderness and love.' And yet…

Gide admitted to being upset that in summertime Moscow everyone dressed in white and looked alike. Sneaking out of the luxurious Metropol Hotel, where his hosts accommodated him in a six-room suite, he was distressed to see people forming long queues in front of stores even before they had opened, in the hope of buying 'repulsive' goods. He was unfavorably struck by the 'inertia' of the masses and the prevalent conformity, by the utter ignorance of foreign countries, by the emergence of a 'petit bourgeois' spirit, by the degradation of artists and writers. The luxury with which his hosts surrounded an honored foreign guest like himself, in such contrast with the prevailing poverty, revolted him.

Although Gide reaffirmed his affection for the Soviet Union, he became at once the object of vicious attacks, which accused him, initially, of 'superficiality' and 'hasty judgements' and, in time, after Moscow had given the appropriate signal, of being a 'Judas' and a Fascist agent. He responded with *Afterthoughts on the U.S.S.R.*, in which he condemned outright what the Communists had done to Russia: the country had 'betrayed all our hopes.'

Although they were mercilessly attacked and slandered by the Communists as 'social Fascists,' European socialists hesitated to respond in kind for fear of giving comfort to the counterrevolution. The Second International, which led a desultory existence during the interwar period, ignored appeals by Russian émigrés to adopt a firm stand against the persecution of fellow socialists in the USSR. They were regarded as poor losers. The 1923 congress of the Second International asserted that any foreign intervention against the USSR would aim not at

> remedying the errors of the current phase of the Russian Revolution, but at destroying the Revolution itself. Far from establishing genuine democracy, it would merely set up a government of bloody counter-revolutionaries to act as a vehicle for the exploitation of the Russian people by Western Imperialism.

One might have expected to find the most determined opponents of Communism in the West among businessmen, but, in fact, many of them turned out to be neutral and even friendly to the Soviet government. For one, they tended to dismiss Communist ideology as fodder for the masses, behind which lurked an elite's commonplace material interests. And even if the Communists believed what they preached, business experience would soon cure them of their utopianism. In 1920, Lloyd George expressed this belief to justify his decision to open commercial talks with Moscow:

> We have failed to restore Russia to sanity by force. I believe we can do it and save her by trade. Commerce has a sobering effect in its operations. The simple sums in addition and subtraction which it inculcates soon dispose of wild theories.[7]

And according to Henry Ford, a reactionary and an anti-Semite, the more the Russians industrialized, the better they would behave because 'rightness in mechanics [and] rightness in morals are basically the same thing.'

Such wishful thinking received reinforcement from commercial self-interest. The international business community regarded Soviet Russia as one of the world's largest potential markets, and when Moscow began its industrialization drive, foreign businessmen, suffering from the Depression, fell over each other to fill orders for Stalin's Five-Year Plans. Some of the grandest enterprises built in the USSR in the 1930s were constructed with the technical advice and under the management of Western firms. It was Ford who built Russia's first automobile factory at Nizhnii Novgorod (Gorky), and Western firms that erected the gigantic iron and steel works at Magnitogorsk in the Urals.

The Nazis rode to power in 1932–33 on a platform in which anti-Semitism and anti-Communism played a central role. Unlike the Soviet Union, which concealed its barbarities behind a wall of near total censorship and which, even as it violated every humanitarian and democratic ideal, proclaimed its adherence to them, the Nazis, operating in the heart of Europe, neither could nor wished to pretend they were anything but noble barbarians. By so doing, they instantly aroused the hostility of opinion leaders in the West; and since the Soviet Union came out – in words, at any rate – against Nazism while Western governments seemed to appease it, Moscow reaped generous benefits. The most effective spies for the Soviet Union before and during World War II were individuals won over by Moscow's anti-Nazi stand.

The relationship between Nazism and Communism was much more complicated than the appearance of their irreconcilable hostility would suggest. The two movements competed fiercely, but they also collaborated.

For one, they had a common enemy, which was liberal democracy with its reverence for civil rights, property, and peace. Both totalitarian regimes regarded human beings as expendable raw material for the construction of a new social order and the creation of a 'new man.' Unlike the Soviet Union, Nazi Germany tolerated private property but treated it as a revokable trust rather than an inherent right, and regulated it minutely for the benefit of the state. Both regimes viewed pacifism with contempt: in Lenin's words, 'the slogan of "peace" … is a slogan of philistines and priests.' After coming to power, Lenin insisted that there could be no coexistence between Communism and 'imperialism': one or the other had to win out, and before that happened, 'a series of the most terrible conflicts between the Soviet republic and the bourgeois states is unavoidable.'[8] As for Hitler, his glorification of militarism and his single-minded preoccupation with building up

Germany's armed forces for war are too well known to require elaboration.

But the affinities between Nazism and Communism ran deeper still. Hitler profited greatly from the existence of the Soviet state, using it both as a threat with which to frighten German voters and as a model to emulate in shaping his dictatorship. One of the factors he exploited in the critical elections of 1932–33, which brought him to power, was the fear of a Communist takeover. At his request, the Reichstag granted him extraordinary powers by blaming on the Communists the fire that had gutted its Berlin building. The Ordinance for the Protection of the People and the State, which provided the legal basis of Hitler's dictatorship until the collapse of the Third Reich in 1945, authorized restrictions on personal liberties and freedom of the press, assembly, and association, as well as confiscations and limitations on property rights. These measures, without other precedents but familiar to the historian of Lenin's Russia, bestowed on the Führer formally the unlimited powers enjoyed de facto by the rulers of the Soviet Union.

Hitler found in the Soviet Union a ready model for the one-party state with which to implement the authority granted him by the March 1933 ordinance. This kind of a state has traditionally been labeled 'totalitarian,' a term popularized by the Italian dictator Benito Mussolini to define his Fascist regime. The totalitarian state aims at obliterating all distinctions between itself and the citizenry (society) by penetrating and controlling every aspect of organized life. It attains this objective with the help of the ruling party, which enjoys a political monopoly and governs with the assistance of a security police endowed with unrestricted powers. In such a state, law is not a means of protecting the individual but a mechanism of governance.

In recent years, some political scientists in the West have rejected the totalitarian model on the grounds that no state has ever succeeded in obtaining the degree of control that the concept implies. Even in Stalin's Russia, so the argument runs, the regime had to contend with diverse interest groups and pay some heed to public opinion. True as these objections may be, they do not invalidate the concept of totalitarianism. All political terms are approximations. In the words of the Harvard political scientist Carl J. Friedrich,

> The argument of historical uniqueness of any configuration does not mean that it is 'wholly' unique; for nothing is. All historical phenomena belong to broad classes of analytic objects....[A] sufficiently variegated pattern of distinctive elements ... constitutes historical uniqueness.[9]

Thus, 'democracy,' which means rule by the people, has long ago been noted to accord special influence to elites and lobbies. There has never existed an untrammeled free market as implied in the concept of capitalism: even at the height of laissez-faire in the mid–nineteenth century, governments in some measure restrained and regulated private enterprise. The same standard should be applied to the totalitarian model.

The ambitions of totalitarian regimes were so vast as to be unattainable in their entirety. But even when only partially realized, they created conditions quite different from those of the most autocratic regimes of premodern times:

Because totalitarian rule strives for the impossible and wants to place at its disposal the personality of man and destiny, it can be realized only in a fragmentary manner. It lies in its being that its goal can never be attained and made total but must remain a tendency, a *claim* to rule. ... Totalitarian rule is not a thoroughly rationalized apparatus, that works with equal effectiveness in all its parts. This is something it would well like to be and in some places it may perhaps approach this ideal, but seen as a whole, its claim to power is realizable only in a diffuse manner, with very different intensities at various times in various realms of life; at the same time, totalitarian and non-totalitarian features are always commingled. But this is precisely why the consequences of the totalitarian claim to power are so dangerous and oppressive, because they are so hazy, so incalculable, and so difficult to demonstrate ... This contortion follows from the unfulfillable aspiration to power: it characterizes life under such a regime and makes it so exceedingly difficult for all outsiders to grasp.[10]

The principal difference between totalitarian regimes of the Communist and 'Fascist' varieties lies in the fact that the former thought globally while the latter focused on the nation: 'Fascist' regimes, too, accepted the notion of class conflict but saw it as one between 'have' and 'have-not' nations. This was articulated by Mussolini in a speech to the Chamber of Deputies in 1921, a year before he seized power. Addressing the Communist deputies, he said:

Between us and the Communists there are no political affinities but there are intellectual ones. Like you, we consider necessary a centralized and unitary state which imposes iron discipline on all persons, with this difference, that you reach this conclusion by way of the concept of class, and we by the way of the concept of nation."

It is one of the paradoxes of history that Communist efforts to subvert the West have had the opposite effect of the one intended. The deliberate splitting of socialist parties weakened the Marxist cause. At the same time, the Soviet example exerted the greatest influence on 'Fascism,' which exploited the Communist threat to frighten the populace into surrendering its rights and emulated the Leninist-Stalinist model to create a totalitarian regime that would nearly destroy the Soviet Union.

Although in the 1930s the Soviet Union and its Communist ideology gained a great deal of sympathy in the West, indications were lacking that this sympathy would translate into power. As noted, Western Communist parties, even where they acquired a solid footing, remained isolated. In 1935, frightened by the rise of anti-Communist, 'Fascist' regimes, Moscow reversed its policy of treating socialists as arch-enemies and ordered Communist parties to enter into alliances with them as well as with all other groups opposed to Fascism. The short-lived Popular Front governments founded in France (1936–37) and Spain (1936–39) did little to bring the Communist parties into the mainstream of political life.

While building up anti-Fascist coalitions, Stalin maintained correct relations with both Mussolini and Hitler, which would culminate in the Nazi-Soviet nonaggression pact of 1939 and the USSR for all practical purposes joining the Axis powers.

The affinity of totalitarian regimes for each other, whether they professed internationalism and Communism, or racism and nationalism, is reflected in the admiration that the leaders of these regimes had for one another. While German and Soviet forces were locked in war, Hitler spoke in a private circle of Stalin's 'genius' and speculated aloud whether or not to join forces with him to destroy the Western democracies.[12] Mao Zedong, a Communist so radical that he considered the Soviet Union to have abandoned the true faith, when criticized at the height of the so-called Cultural Revolution for causing the death of so many Communist comrades, responded: 'Look at World War II, at Hitler's cruelty. The more cruelty, the more enthusiasm for revolution.'[13]

World War II, in which Stalin bought victory by the lavish expenditure of his subjects' lives, did not bring him control of Europe. But he did emerge from it in possession of most of the continent's eastern half, which his troops occupied and on which they imposed Communist regimes. For two or three years after the end of the war, Stalin allowed these countries a certain measure of political diversity under Communist control. But after 1948, when Josip Broz Tito, the Communist ruler of Yugoslavia, asserted his independence from Moscow and broke with it, Stalin imposed on his East European dependencies one-party rule. Poland, Czechoslovakia, Hungary, East Germany, Romania, and Bulgaria, though nominally sovereign, were, in fact, with minor deviations, 'satellites' – clones of the Soviet state and completely subservient to it, especially in matters of foreign policy. The Soviet empire was now expanded into the Soviet bloc.

The West, by and large, acquiesced to Soviet domination of most of Eastern Europe since it could do nothing about it. It tacitly acknowledged a Soviet sphere of influence in that region, and had Moscow been satisfied with its post-World War II gains, relations between East and West might have stabilized. If, however, such gains led to what came to be known as the Cold War, it was because Communism by its very nature could not remain stable and content: it needed crises and it needed expansion.

The wartime alliance began to break down in the closing phases of World War II, when the war's outcome was no longer in doubt. It disintegrated in 1945–46, after Moscow had renounced its 1925 nonaggression treaty with Turkey and made on Turkey unacceptable territorial demands. Shortly afterward, the Communists launched a civil war in Greece. Britain came to the defense of the two countries, but, exhausted by the war, it could not do so for long. In 1947, on the initiative of President Harry Truman, the task of containing the USSR was assumed by the United States, first by means of the so-called Truman Doctrine of aid to Turkey and Greece (March 1947) and then by the device of the Marshall Plan (June–July 1947), which provided substantial financial aid for the reconstruction of Western Europe. In April 1949, the United States took the unprecedented step of entering into a defensive alliance with ten West European states and Canada for mutual assistance against external aggression, implicitly by the Soviet bloc (the North Atlantic Treaty Organization, or NATO). NATO's headquarters were located in Paris, and its first supreme command went to the American general Dwight D. Eisenhower. After Communist North Korea invaded South Korea in June 1950, at what was then suspected and now is known to have been Moscow's initiative, the Allies declared West Germany a sovereign nation and invited her to join NATO (May 1955). Moscow at once responded with the creation of the Warsaw Pact of eight European Communist states. The Cold War was institutionalized.

A great deal of ink has been spilled on the history of the Cold War. Some historians place the blame for it on the United States and its allies; others distribute the responsibility between East and West. It cannot be denied that the West, notably the United States, the undisputed leader of the alliance, occasionally overreacted to the Communist threat: whatever threat the Communist bloc posed to the global balance of power, there was never the slightest danger of a Communist takeover of the United States. Yet now that passions have cooled, it is difficult to avoid the conclusion that the overwhelming responsibility for the Cold War lay with Moscow. After all, Moscow proclaimed, loud and clear, its intention to promote everywhere civil wars and to impose everywhere Communist regimes; Article 17 of the twenty-one-point rules of admission to the Comintern stated explicitly, 'The Communist International has declared war on the entire bourgeois world.' The USSR carried out this threat wherever the opportunity presented itself, even when, in the midst of World War II, to placate its new Western allies, it dissolved the Comintern.

And if further proof is needed, it is significant that as soon as the Soviet Union dissolved and power in Russia passed to a democratically elected government that disowned Communism, the Cold War suddenly ceased. The new president of Russia, Boris Yeltsin, in a June 1992 address to the American House of Representatives, declared:

> The world can sigh in relief. The idol of Communism, which spread everywhere social strife, animosity and unparalleled brutality, which instilled fear in humanity, has collapsed. It has collapsed never to rise again.[14]

Yeltsin, at least, seemed to have had no doubt who was behind the Cold War.

Communism spawned various terrorist movements that had little if anything to do with Marxism or socialism; they served mainly to cover up criminal activities: abductions, extortions, murder. Typical of this genre, widespread in the 1970s, were such organizations as the Baader-Meinhof group in Germany (known now to have been supported by the East German secret police), Italy's Red Brigades, the French Action Directe, and the Japanese Red Army. Composed of small groups of intellectuals, these parties carried out terror operations against prominent businessmen and politicians with the intention of bringing down 'capitalism.' All were sooner or later liquidated.

These anarchist outrages, inspired by Third World leaders like Mao Zedong and Che Guevara, reflected the frustration of fanatics with the seemingly accommodationist course vis-à-vis the capitalist West adopted by the post-Stalinist Soviet leadership. The main trend of European radical politics proceeded in the opposite direction, namely the adaptation of Communism to contemporary reality. Its principal manifestation was the movement that emerged in the 1970s under the name Eurocommunism.

Immediately after World War II, European Communists, benefiting from the enormous prestige the Soviet Union had acquired for its contribution to victory, gained new adherents. In some European states they joined coalition governments. But in the 1950s and 1960s their following melted away. A variety of factors contributed to this decline: Khrushchev's revelations of Stalin's barbarities, the military suppression of the Hungarian and Czechoslovak attempts at devising their own form of Communism, and the identification of Communism with anti-Semitic persecution, especially in Poland.

Eurocommunism was an attempt to broaden Communism's electoral appeal by disassociating it from its identification with Soviet repression and economic backwardness. The Eurocommunists, especially strong among intellectuals in France, Spain, and Italy, wanted to pursue a path more in conformity with Europe's political traditions. Santiago Carrillo, the general secretary of the Spanish Communist Party, defined the movement's objectives in 1976 as follows:

> The parties included in the 'Eurocommunist' trend are agreed on the need to advance to socialism with democracy, a multi-party system, parliaments and representative institutions, sovereignty of the people regularly exercised through universal suffrage, trade unions independent of the State, freedom for the opposition, human rights, religious freedom, freedom for cultural, scientific and artistic creation, and the development of the

broadest forms of popular participation at all levels and in all branches of social activity.

These were admirable sentiments, but every one of them would have been anathema to Lenin. Hence it is incorrect to describe this movement as a 'moderate version of Communism': the short-lived and unsuccessful attempt to bring Communism into the mainstream of political life really meant a repudiation of everything that Communism stood for.

Eurocommunism proved a flash in the pan. In the 1980s, the Communist parties throughout Europe found themselves once again marginalized. Their most powerful showing was in Italy and France, where in parliamentary elections of 1978–79 they gained 30.4 and 20.6 percent of the vote, respectively. In the most industrialized countries of Europe, however, their share of the vote remained minuscule: 0.05 percent in the United Kingdom and 0.3 percent in West Germany.[15] And the trend pointed downward.

After the Soviet Union had collapsed, the European Communists underwent many changes and splits. The hard-line parties and factions attributed the collapse to Gorbachev's compromises with capitalism and continued to adhere to Stalinism. Others turned their back on traditional Communism. Thus, the Italian Communist Party, the most numerous and least doctrinaire, quietly renamed itself the Democratic Party of the Left. Most of the others similarly shed their Communist appellations and symbols.

Communism proved a no-win proposition: Western political culture militated against the crudities of an ideology that, even if Western in origin, acquired shape in a non-Western environment. Western Communism dissolved in social democracy before surrendering to capitalism, and then virtually vanished from the scene.

V *The Third World*

Every Communist country or Party has its own specific history and its own particular regional and local variations, but a linkage can always be traced to the pattern elaborated in Moscow in November 1917. This linkage forms a sort of genetic code of Communism.[1]

The linkage alluded to in the above citation derives from the fact that Communism everywhere came into existence in one of two ways: either imposed by the Soviet army (as in Eastern Europe) or else emerging, usually with Soviet help, in countries whose political culture (an absence of established traditions of private property and rule of law, a heritage of autocracy, etc.) as well as social structure (preponderance of peasantry, weakly developed middle class) resembled those of pre-1917 Russia. Although designed for advanced industrial societies, in practice Communism struck root only in underdeveloped agrarian societies. Hence the recurrent pattern.

The features of Marxism-Leninism that such countries copied were: 1) rule by a single, monopolistic party organized along military lines and owed unquestioned obedience; 2) this rule being exercised without any external restraints; 3) the abolition of private property in the means of production and the concurrent nationalization of all human and material resources; 4) disregard of human rights. Such regimes insisted that the party was omniscient and omnipotent: it was always right; it acknowledged no limits to its power. In nearly all cases, the 'party' was embodied in a leader who personified the cause and came to be deified.

Conventional wisdom holds that poverty breeds Communism. Reality is different: poor countries do not opt for Communism. Nowhere in the world has a poor majority, or any majority for that matter, voted the Communists into power. Rather, poor countries are less able to resist Communist takeovers because they lack the institutions that in richer, more advanced societies thwart aspiring radical dictators. It is the absence of institutions making for affluence, especially the rights of property and the rule of law, that keeps countries poor and, at the same time, makes them vulnerable to dictatorships, whether of the left or right variety. In the words of a student of the Cambodian Communist regime, the most extreme on record, 'the absence of effective intermediary structures between the people and their successive leaders predisposed the society to the unrestrained exercise of power.'[2] Thus, the same factors that keep countries poor – above all, lawlessness – facilitate Communist takeovers.

These factors have a further effect. In the Orient, since the earliest times, the absence of private property in land meant that distinction and affluence could be gained in one way only: by acquiring prominence in the sovereign's employ. Government posts, consequently, were viewed not as service to the country but as a means of personal enrichment. It was natural, therefore, that participation in Communist regimes, which concentrated all power and all wealth in their hands, was perceived as the principal means of gaining status as well as fortune. (This, of course, held true also in Russia.)

In the early years of the twentieth century, European socialists wondered why capitalism did not collapse as Marx and Engels had predicted. The Revisionists resolved the problem by acknowledging that Marx and Engels had been mistaken on this particular point. For orthodox Marxists, however, this was not an acceptable solution, because the doctrine, said to be scientific, could tolerate no deviations or exceptions: it stood or fell as a whole.

Confronting this problem, Lenin drew on the work of the English economist J. A. Hobson, who in his *Imperialism* (1902) explained the colonial drives of the time as the result of the capitalists' quest for new markets for their goods and new outlets for their capital. Lenin elaborated this thesis in his *Imperialism, the Highest Stage of Capitalism* (1916–17), in which he argued that the colonies were essential to the survival of advanced capitalism by propping up its ailing economies and enabling it to buy off the working class. An assault on the imperial possessions of the great powers was therefore an indispensable component of modern revolutionary strategy.

The difficulty with this plan was that the colonies, as well as the semicolonial dependencies of the capitalist countries in Asia, Africa, and Latin America, had few if any industries and therefore no significant industrial proletariat. Lenin sought to resolve the predicament of promoting a proletarian revolution in countries without an industrial base by asking the Second Congress of the Comintern to adopt a colonial program based on two premises: 1) that these regions could bypass the capitalist stage and proceed directly from 'feudalism' to social-ism; and 2) that the Communists active there forge an alliance (temporary, of course) with the native 'nationalist bourgeoisie' against foreign imperialists.

Lenin's proposals aroused considerable opposition from the handful of Comintern delegates representing the colonial regions, who found their native bourgeoisie no less odious than they did foreign imperialists. But Lenin held his ground, and the Comintern committed itself to what came to be known as wars of 'national liberation,' in which the Communists, while retaining their distinct identity, championed the nationalist cause and collaborated with other anti-imperialist groups.

Attempts to implement this policy invariably failed: instead of exploiting the nationalists for their own purposes, the Communists found themselves exploited by them.

In 1918–19, Allied armies occupied western Anatolia and Constantinople, the capital of the Ottoman Empire, a defeated partner of Germany in World War I. Expelling these foreigners became the avowed mission of a Turkish nationalist move-ment, headed by Kemal Pasha (Atatürk). In 1920, Kemal pro-posed to Moscow collaboration against the occupying powers. Moscow readily agreed and in 1921 signed with him a Treaty of Friendship, committing the two countries to pursue jointly the struggle against 'imperialism.' Following Comintern practice, Moscow accompanied this state-to-state collaboration with subversive activity. A recently declassified document from the Soviet Communist Party's archive reveals that even as it was publicly embracing the Turkish nationalists, Moscow secretly plotted to overthrow them. Drafted by Lenin, the directive, from late 1920, reads as follows:

> Do not trust the Kemalists; do not give them arms; concentrate
> all efforts on Soviet agitation among the Turks and on the build-
> ing in Turkey of a solid Soviet party capable of triumphing
> through its own efforts.[3]

Kemal, for his part, while welcoming Moscow's help and planning to found a one-party state on the Soviet model, had no
intention of tolerating Communists on Turkish soil. Two
months after a Comintern agent had organized the Turkish
Communist Party, the agent and his associates were found
dead, almost certainly murdered by the Kemalists.

A fiasco on a much grander scale but similar in nature met
Soviet policies in China. China was highly important to the
Comintern and unusually promising. The most populous
country in the world, it had been ruthlessly exploited by the
European powers and Japan. The exploitation gave rise to xenophobia: China seethed with hostility toward foreigners, which
periodically erupted into violence. Sun Yat-sen, the head of the
Nationalist Party, or Kuomintang, which had ruled China
since 1911–12, admired the Soviet Union for having shaken off
foreign economic and political domination. Although primarily an agricultural country, China also had a working class
employed mostly in light industry and concentrated in
Shanghai. Lenin placed great hopes on China, even if he
undoubtedly engaged in hyperbole when he told a visiting
diplomatic mission from Peking that 'the Chinese revolution
… will finally bring about the downfall of world imperialism.'

Chiang Kai-shek, who emerged as the leading figure in the
Kuomintang during the 1920s, was greatly impressed by the
Soviet example and welcomed Soviet 'advisers,' who poured

into China. The Chinese Communist Party, formed in 1921 on Moscow's directives and made up almost exclusively of literati and students, retained its separate identity, as the Comintern rules required, but after 1923 many of its members enrolled individually in the Kuomintang. This they did on orders from Moscow, which hoped in this manner to build up in China an anti-imperialist front. To this end, it offered the Kuomintang military and political advice. Disagreements between the two partners proliferated, however, especially after 1925, when Sun Yat-sen died and Chiang Kai-shek took charge. In April 1927, Chiang expelled the Communists from his party and had thousands of them killed.

Stalin deduced from this debacle that it was futile to attempt to harness Third World nationalism for Communist purposes. On these grounds, in 1928, at its Sixth Congress, the Comintern abandoned the policy of lending support to the 'national bourgeoisie.' Henceforth, until Stalin's death twenty-five years later, the USSR sharply reduced its activities in the colonial and quasi-colonial regions. In the process, it abandoned collaboration with the native 'bourgeoisie,' whom it came to regard, even after their countries had gained independence, as 'lackeys' of the imperial powers. Thus in 1953 the *Great Soviet Encyclopedia* described Mahatma Gandhi as an 'agent of British Imperialism.' Instead, the USSR relied on the Communist parties, whether legal or illegal, regardless of how small they were. In 1948 Moscow instigated a series of Communist armed revolts in southeast Asia – Burma, Malaya, Indonesia, and the Philippines – all of which were suppressed. The Communists succeeded only in Indochina (Vietnam), where in 1954 a native guerrilla army expelled the French from the northern half of the country. As long as Stalin was alive, the foreign policy of the USSR was concentrated on building up its own industrial and military might and sowing dissent among the Great Powers.

On the face of it, the 1949 victory of the Chinese Communists over the Kuomintang and their conquest of all of mainland China represented an immense triumph for the Communist cause. All of a sudden, the Marxist-Leninist movement spread to half a billion people, nearly twice the number previously living under its rule. But this triumph turned out to be a mixed blessing, for it was purchased at the price of the movement's international unity: Communist China soon went its own way, splitting the movement. Nationalism once again triumphed over class allegiance.

In October 1927, what was left of the Chinese Communist organization after Chiang Kai-shek's crackdown retreated into the rural hinterland. Mao Zedong (Mao Tse-tung), one of its leaders, once an ardent supporter of the Kuomintang, spent the following twenty years in the political wilderness, building up a guerrilla army. In 1931, the Chinese Communists proclaimed a Chinese Soviet republic. Neither then nor during World War II, however, did Stalin show any inclination to support them. For one, he was more concerned with safeguarding the interests of the USSR in the Far East than in promoting Communism there; and the interests of the USSR required a strong, unified China, able to contain Japan. In Stalin's eyes, the Kuomintang was much better suited for this role, for which reason he preferred to subsidize Chiang. Later, Stalin was mindful of his experience with an independent Communist

Party in Yugoslavia, which in 1948 under the leadership of Josip (Broz) Tito had refused to obey Moscow's orders and had broken with it. Apprehensive lest China develop into another 'Titoist' state, Stalin tried to persuade Mao to come to terms with Chiang. Mao ignored this advice and proceeded, at the head of a peasant army, to conquer all of China.

Stalin continued to patronize Mao even after the latter had become the undisputed master of China. Mao was so dependent on the USSR for economic and military support that for the time being he had to swallow his pride and accept the Soviet Union as a leader and model. But with the advent of Khrushchev Mao's attitude changed, because he perceived Stalin's successors as traitors to the cause. In 1959 relations between Moscow and Beijing reached a near breaking point, in large part because of Moscow's refusal to share with Beijing nuclear technology. The following year Khrushchev unilaterally withdrew Soviet technical advisers from China.

Mao soon developed an idiosyncratic variant of Communism. In the words of a leading authority on the subject, the 'dominant values' of Mao's ideology 'seem completely alien to Marxism': it merely serves to illustrate 'the unlimited flexibility of any doctrine once it becomes historically influential.'[4] On nearly every important issue, Mao stood Marx on his head. Instead of relying on industrial workers to make revolution, he elevated the peasantry to the rank of the leading revolutionary class: the world revolution, he asserted, would be accomplished not by Europeans (among whom he included Russians) but by the peoples of Asia, Africa, and Latin America. He also rejected Marx's adage 'It is not consciousness that determines life, but life that determines consciousness,'[5] i.e., coping with material necessities defines how humans think and feel. Instead Mao insisted that ideas shape behavior: 'objective factors' that Marxism treated as decisive were for Mao a 'bourgeois' concept. They could never thwart the masses once they had made up their mind to accomplish something. Knowledge was, therefore, potentially evil because it inhibited resolve; for this reason it was harmful to read too much. The new society and the new man would be created not by altered economic and social conditions but by changes in the cultural and intellectual 'superstructure.' This was revisionism of a particular kind: whereas Western Revisionism, derived from Eduard Bernstein, sought to rectify Marx's doctrines by adapting them to reality, Mao's revisionism chose to disregard reality.

Such unorthodox ideas led to a falling out with Moscow. At the Twentieth Party Congress Moscow approved the policy of détente with the West and declared war to be no longer necessary for Communism's global triumph, on the grounds that the world was inexorably shifting to Communism. Mao objected to this course, convinced that the Soviet acquisition of intercontinental missiles warranted an aggressive policy toward the capitalist West. Like Lenin, Mao felt that wars with capitalism were unavoidable. He rejected Khrushchev's doctrine, according to which Communism could prevail without violence, by parliamentary means. He favored violence. ('War is the highest form of struggle for resolving contradictions'; 'Political power grows out of the barrel of a gun.')[6]

Hence Mao spurned the argument that the invention of thermonuclear weapons eliminated war as a political option. He dismissed the atom bomb as a 'paper tiger which the U.S. reactionaries use to scare people. It looks terrible, but in fact it isn't."[7] He further repudiated as treasonous the policy of arms-control agreements inaugurated in 1968, and he scoffed at the idea that a thermonuclear war would mean the extinction of life on earth. With astonishing insouciance, he wrote:

> If worst came to the worst and half of mankind died, the other half would remain while imperialism would be razed to the ground and the whole world would become socialist; in a number of years there would be 2,700 million people again and definitely more.[8]

Adhering to the Stalinist line, he rejected the post-Stalinist strategy of supporting ex-colonial regimes like Nehru's in India and Nasser's in Egypt.

But the fundamental cause of the mounting conflict, which in 1969 produced clashes along the Sino-Soviet border, involved not strategy and tactics, important as these were, but hegemony in the world's Communist movement. Moscow had always insisted that it was the movement's undisputed leader; this claim was formalized in the 1920 statutes of the Comintern and never abandoned. In an off-the-record speech in Warsaw in 1956, Khrushchev revealed that Stalin had told Mao that Moscow must have the final word on all matters concerning the Communist camp. After 1956, Mao refused to play by these rules, because, as noted, he regarded Stalin's successors as traitors to Marxism-Leninism. He now saw himself not only as an equal to Moscow's rulers but as their superior. Even before he had become ruler of China, he claimed for himself authorship of a Marxist doctrine designed for the world's non-Western countries, in which revolutions would be made by the peasantry. As early as 1945, one of Mao's close associates claimed, 'Mao Tse-tung's great accomplishment has been to change Marxism from a European to an Asian form' that would guide a great part of humanity living under the same conditions as the Chinese. Later, in seeking to elbow the Soviet Union out of Africa, Beijing resorted to racist arguments, charging that the Russians, being 'white,' could not possibly understand either Orientals or Africans. Mao was celebrated at home as the prophet of the true faith. Not untypical was the title of a book published in Beijing in 1966: *The Brilliance of Mao Tse-tung's Thought Illuminates the Whole World.* Thus, 'what began as a dispute over alternative revolutionary strategies...developed into an incipient struggle for power in the international Communist movement.'[9]

The Sino-Soviet conflict revealed an elemental and irremediable weakness of the Communist cause. It demonstrated that foreign Communists were prepared to follow Moscow's leadership only as long as they lacked a significant domestic base and depended on Moscow for financial and military assistance. But under these conditions they were marginalized and powerless. If they succeeded in acquiring significant support at home, as happened first in Yugoslavia and then in China, they turned into an autonomous political force and hence an asset to international Communism, but then they no longer wanted to take orders from the Russians or acknowledge the national interests of the Soviet Union as supreme. The result was a dilemma: the more successful foreign Communists were, the more independent they became and the less able was Moscow to control them. Moscow, therefore, had to choose between its own interests and those of the international movement. If the Soviet leadership was serious about spreading Communism, then it had to give up its claims to leadership and abandon the theory that the interests of Communism and the interests of the Soviet Union were one and the same. But then the international movement would become fragmented and subject to centrifugal forces, thereby losing what to Lenin was the essential feature of his regime: rigorous centralism.

The strategy of assisting anti-imperialist forces in the Third World, adopted by Stalin's successors after his death, appeared much more feasible in the 1950s than it had been thirty years earlier, because after World War II the imperial powers had granted independence to most of their colonies. Among them were such populous and strategically located countries as India, Indonesia, and Egypt. They were governed by inexperienced nationalist leaders, usually short of money, who viewed political sovereignty as merely a first step to genuine independence based on economic self-sufficiency. They admired the Soviet Union as a country that had emerged from backwardness into industrial might; desiring to emulate it, they welcomed Soviet counsel and assistance. In some cases, aspiring dictators also saw in the Soviet Union assurance that they would stay in power: in return for proclaiming themselves 'socialist,' they obtained the help of the Communist bloc's security organs and armed forces against domestic and foreign rivals.

After 1956, Moscow engaged itself actively in the Third World, seeking to build up an alliance embracing half of the world's population against the West, notably the United States. The means of securing a foothold varied. In India, it financed and supervised the construction of a giant steel mill; elsewhere it built power stations and bakeries. In Egypt, Moscow helped construct the Aswan Dam, which for the first time made it possible to control the annual flooding of the Nile. Such actions were meant to contrast with the 'selfish' behavior of the capitalist West. Moscow armed the Arabs against Israel and Ethiopia against Somalia. In all these cases, Soviet 'advisers' accompanied the aid, enabling Moscow to establish a world-wide physical presence. Aid also created an economic dependency that could be translated into political dependency.

In the end, this ambitious and costly policy brought very modest rewards. The Soviet Union simply lacked the economic resources to play the kind of role called for by its new Third World policy. In country after country, from the Middle East to Africa, Moscow rushed to exploit power vacuums, extending financial and military assistance, only to find that an unforeseen event had removed its ally, or else he had changed his mind. As someone said, Third World leaders could not be bought; they could only be rented.

The principal effect of Moscow's Third World activities was to alarm the West and exacerbate the Cold War. They also heavily strained its treasury.

Marxist-Leninists, regarding their doctrine as a science, tried to analyze their experiences and learn from their mistakes, not so much as concerned the movement's ultimate objective, which remained beyond criticism, but its strategy and tactics. Lenin learned from Marx that to prevent a counterrevolution he had ruthlessly to demolish the entire institutional structure of capitalism. Observing the Revisionism of Stalin's successors, Mao concluded that demolishing institutions was not enough: one had to change man. Changing human beings was, of course, the ultimate objective of Marxism. But Mao decided that it had to be realized without delay, and he committed his entire rule to make it reality.

The Chinese Communists established a totalitarian regime closely modeled on the Soviet. Initially, Mao also faithfully copied Stalin's economic policies, collectivizing agriculture and introducing Five-Year Plans of industrialization. But there were differences. One of them was that whereas the Soviet dictatorship, the heir of tsarism, did not much care what people thought as long as they conformed and pretended to believe, the Chinese Communists were determined to attain genuine intellectual and spiritual conformity.* This aspiration was rooted in Confucianism, which laid stress on moral perfectibility and demanded that government rest on moral virtue rather than mere coercion. But it was immediately inspired by Mao's fear that unless his subjects' minds were reshaped so that they fully assimilated the doctrines of Marx, Lenin, and Mao himself, China would suffer the same fate as Soviet Russia – i.e., turn Revisionist and abandon the true faith.

Mao's premises led to fantastic experiments, all of which miscarried, at great cost in human lives and to the nation's well-being. Chinese citizens, especially intellectuals, suspected of holding anachronistic or subversive thoughts were subjected to systematic 'reeducation,' often in concentration camps, in which they were exposed to what has been aptly

---

* Many observers regarded forcible indoctrination as an essential feature of Soviet Communism. This misconception may have been due to the fact that for the first forty years of the regime foreigners obtained virtually all their knowledge of the USSR from Soviet sources, and these stressed uniformity of thought and total commitment to Communist ideology. Reality was quite different.

called 'brainwashing.' It was mental torture designed to break the spirit.

The same assumptions also spawned the so-called Great Leap Forward, launched in 1958. Inspired by the desire to demonstrate to the world that China had found a better and speedier way to overcome economic backwardness than the Russians, Mao declared that China's goal was to surpass in five years Britain's output of coal and steel. This was to be accomplished by over half a billion people, who were herded into twenty-four thousand 'people's communes,' which combined primitive household industrial pursuits with agriculture. A perfect example of Mao's willingness to ignore economic reality, it rested on the theorem, spelled out in *Quotations from Chairman Mao* (popularly referred to as Mao's *Little Red Book*), which for a time was the only book available in China, that the Chinese people were a tabula rasa:

> Apart from their other characteristics, the outstanding thing about China's 600 million people is that they are 'poor and blank.' This may seem a bad thing, but in reality it is a good thing. Poverty gives rise to the desire for change, the desire for action and the desire for revolution. On a blank sheet of paper free from any mark, the freshest and most beautiful characters can be written, the freshest and most beautiful pictures can be painted.[10]

This was said of a nation that had behind it thousands of years of statehood.

There was to be no limit to what humans could accomplish once they set their mind to it: one slogan of the Great Leap Forward pledged, 'We shall teach the sun and moon to change places. We shall create a new heaven and earth for man.' Thus Marxism, which to its founders was a strictly materialist doctrine, turned in the hands of China's self-proclaimed Marxist dictator into a utopian idealism that subordinated reality to the human will.

The Great Leap wrought such economic chaos that it had to be abandoned. Its cost in human lives was staggering: American demographers, given access to population statistics after Mao's death, determined that at least 30 million Chinese perished in a famine of which the outside world had not even been aware.[11] But failure did not discourage Mao, as his megalomania reached pathological dimensions. Feeling increasingly isolated from his own party, he launched in 1966 another bizarre and disruptive campaign, this time directed against intellectuals and party officials, who, he feared, would lead China along the same treacherous path that the Soviet Union had followed. This crusade recruited urban youths into the Red Guards to carry out what was officially labeled the Great Proletarian Cultural Revolution but which is more accurately described as a vicious cultural counterrevolution. It was an occurrence without precedent in which a ruler, driven partly by his desire to reignite revolutionary zeal and partly by *folie de grandeur*, brought the country's cultural life to a standstill. For several years China, one of the oldest civilizations in the world, was ravaged by barbarian hordes who had been taught to treat everything beyond their understanding as fit for destruction. At its height, all schools were closed and no books were available except for textbooks and Mao's own works. Performances of Western music were forbidden. The Red Guards assaulted intellectuals and forced them to humiliate themselves publicly; they tortured and killed many of them. Thousands of party officials suffered similar treatment. This anti-intellectual frenzy was brought to a halt only with Mao's death in 1976. Its consequences were not only to deprive an entire generation of an education but also to eviscerate it morally and psychologically.

Although anyone in China who dared to criticize either the Great Leap Forward or the Cultural Revolution risked immediate imprisonment, not a few radical intellectuals in the West sympathized with Mao's barbarities and sought wisdom in his insipid writings.

Mao's successor, Deng Xiaoping, put an end to the wild experimentation. In 1979, he initiated a policy of free-market reforms, which revived the entrepreneurial spirit. Since then, China, although Communist in ideology and form of government, has taken the path of economic privatization that, in effect, meant the abandonment of the most fundamental precept of Communism, the abolition of private property.

Revolutionary movements and regimes tend, up to a point, to grow more radical and more ruthless. This happens because, after successive failures, their leaders, rather than reexamine their fundamental premises, since these provide the rationale for their existence, prefer to implement them more ruthlessly in the conviction that failure was due to insufficient resolve. Ultimately, when nothing succeeds, fatigue sets in and the heirs of the founding fathers settle down to enjoy life, but not before resorting to the most extreme forms of inhumanity.

Just as the Holocaust expressed the quintessential nature of National Socialism, so did the Khmer Rouge rule in Cambodia

(1975–78) represent the purest embodiment of Communism: what it turns into when pushed to its logical conclusion. Its leaders would stop at nothing to attain their objective, which was to create the first truly egalitarian society in the world: to this end they were prepared to annihilate as many of their people as they deemed necessary. It was the most extreme manifestation of the hubris inherent in Communist ideology, the belief in the boundless power of an intellectual elite guided by the Marxist doctrine, with resort to unrestrained violence in order completely to reshape life. The result was devastation on an unimaginable scale.

The leaders of the Khmer Rouge received their higher education in Paris, where they absorbed Rousseau's vision of 'natural man,' as well as the exhortations of Frantz Fanon and Jean-Paul Sartre to violence in the struggle against colonialism. ('One must kill,' Sartre wrote. 'To bring down a European is to … suppress at the same time the oppressor and the oppressed.') On their return to Cambodia, they organized in the northeastern hills a tightly disciplined armed force made up largely of illiterate and semiliterate youths recruited from the poorest peasantry. These troops, for the most part twelve- to fourteen-year-old adolescents, were given intense indoctrination in hatred of all those different from themselves, especially city dwellers and the Vietnamese minority. To develop a 'love of killing and consequently war,' they were trained, like the Nazi SS, in tormenting and slaughtering animals.

Their time came in early 1975, when the Khmer Rouge overthrew the government of Lon Nol, installed by the Americans, and occupied the country's capital, Phnom Penh. The population at large had no inkling what lay in store, because in their propaganda the Khmer Rouge promised to pardon servants of the old regime, rallying all classes against the 'imperialists' and landowners. Yet the instant Khmer Rouge troops entered Phnom Penh, they resorted to the most radical punitive measures. Convinced that cities were the nidus of all evil – in Fanon's words, the home of 'traitors and knaves' – the Khmer Rouge ordered the capital, with its 2.5 million inhabitants, and all other urban centers to be totally evacuated. The victims, driven into the countryside, were allowed to salvage only what they could carry on their backs. Within one week all Cambodian cities were emptied. Four million people, or 60 percent of the population, suffered exile, compelled to live under the most trying conditions, over-worked as well as undernourished. Secondary and higher schools were shut down.

Then the carnage began. Unlike Mao, whom he admired and followed in many respects, the leader of the Khmer Rouge, Pol Pot, did not waste time on 'reeducation' but proceeded directly to the extermination of those categories of the population whom he suspected of actual or potential hostility to the new order: all civilian and military employees of the old regime, former landowners, teachers, merchants, Buddhist monks, and even skilled workers. Members of these groups, officially rele-gated to the lowest class of citizens and deprived of all rights, including access to food rations, were either summarily shot or sent to perform forced labor until they dropped dead from exhaustion. These condemned unfortunates constituted, poten-tially, over two-thirds of the population. They were systemati-cally arrested, interrogated, and tortured until they implicated others, and then executed. The executions involved entire families, including small children, for Pol Pot believed that dissenting ideas and attitudes, derived from one's social position, education, or occupation, were 'evil microbes' that spread like disease. Members of the Communist Party, considered susceptible to contagion, were also subject to liquidation. After the Vietnamese expelled the Khmer Rouge from Cambodia, they discovered mountains of skulls of its victims.

The peasants were not spared, being driven into 'cooperatives' modeled on the Chinese. The state appropriated all the food produced by these communes and, as in pharaonic Egypt, having stored it in temples and other government depositories, doled it out at its discretion. These measures upset traditional rural practices and led to food shortages that in 1978–79, following an unusually severe drought, produced a massive famine.

The killings intensified throughout the forty-four months that the Khmer Rouge controlled Cambodia. People were executed for such offenses as being late to work, complaining about food, criticizing the government, or engaging in premarital sex. In sadism, the brutalities were fully comparable to those perpetrated by the Nazis. Thus on the Vietnamese border

> Khmer Rouge soldiers would rape a Vietnamese woman, then ram a stake or bayonet into her vagina. Pregnant women were cut open, their unborn babies yanked out and slapped against the dying mother's face. The *Yotheas* [youths] also enjoyed cutting the breasts off well endowed Vietnamese women.[12]

Cases were reported of children being ordered to kill their parents.

The toll of these massacres was appalling. According to

reliable estimates, the population of Cambodia at the time the Khmer Rouge seized power in 1975 was 7.3 million; when the Vietnamese took over in 1978, it had declined to 5.8 million. Allowing for the natural population increase during the intervening four years, it should have been over 8 million.[13] In other words, the Pol Pot regime was responsible for the death or population deficit of some 2 million Cambodian citizens, or over one-quarter of the population. These victims represented the best educated and most skilled elements of the nation. The gruesome experiment has been characterized as a 'human tragedy of almost unprecedented proportions [that] occurred because political theoreticians carried out their grand design on the unsuspecting Khmer people.'[14]*

It may be noted that there were no demonstrations anywhere in the world against these outrages and the United Nations passed no resolutions condemning them. The world took them in its stride, presumably because they were committed in what was heralded as a noble cause.

The Marxist regime of Salvador Allende in Chile in 1970–73 presents an unusual case of a Communist revolution attempted in a democratic country by democratic means.

In the 1960s the government of Chile was controlled by Christian Democrats, whose leader, Eduardo Frei, pursued fairly radical social and economic policies. In particular, Frei

---

* Some Western intellectuals, unwilling to blame this unprecedented slaughter on the Communists, attributed it to the Americans, who in 1969–73 had bombed Cambodia in an attempt to destroy the Vietcong forces that had sought refuge there. It is difficult to see, however, why the Cambodians' rage against the Americans would vent itself in the killing of 2 million of their own people.

carried out an ambitious agrarian reform program that called for the expropriation, with compensation, of large estates. Frei also nationalized much of the mining industry. These measures had the effect of polarizing Chilean society between the right, which thought they went too far, and the left, which saw them as inadequate. The popularity of the Frei administration was further undermined by inflation, which on the eve of the 1970 presidential election rose to 35 percent.

In that election, the three leading candidates ran neck and neck. The largest number of votes (36.3 percent) was cast for Salvador Allende, a medical doctor of Marxist sympathies, who represented the Popular Unity Party, a bloc of socialists and Communists. The conservative runner-up received 34.9 percent of the vote. Because no candidate had won an absolute majority, the issue was referred to the Congress. During the two months that followed the election, Allende struck a deal with the Christian Democrats, who agreed to support his candidacy provided he subscribed to a set of conditions committing him to honor Chile's constitution. These included respect for law and political pluralism. Spelled out in the Statute of Constitutional Guarantees, passed by Congress, it enabled Allende to assume the presidency.

Allende's 'Chilean Road to Socialism' was thus from the beginning subject to restraints that impeded the radical designs of its socialist and Communist constituency. Despite his admiration for Fidel Castro, Allende was a romantic idealist rather than a fanatical revolutionary. But his doctrinaire backers, determined to introduce into Chile a 'dictatorship of the proletariat' on the Soviet model, kept pushing him to the left, and as his measures failed, he became radicalized. Allende believed that he could achieve socialist objectives by legal means on the assumption that his reforms would in time gain him the support of the nation's majority. The Communists supported this strategy, convinced that in Chile their objectives could be attained peacefully. Unfortunately for them, this did not happen, in part because Allende's socialist legislation alienated much of the country, and in part because it reduced the country's economy to shambles.

After assuming the presidency, Allende entrusted the economic ministries in his 'United Popular Government' to Communists, who proceeded to nationalize the remaining mining industries, banking, and much of manufacturing. Enacted by decree, these measures bypassed the legislature. The confiscation of the Anaconda and Kennecott copper mines caused foreign investments to dry up. The Soviet Union came to Allende's assistance, extending to him over half a billion dollars in loans. Other countries also offered aid, but it was not enough to rescue Chile's battered finances. To pay for the various social measures, including hikes in wages, the government resorted to the printing presses, which produced an inflation that far surpassed anything seen under Frei: in the three years of Allende's presidency, the value of the currency in circulation increased by a factor of fifteen, and inflation exceeded 300 percent a year.

Concurrently with the nationalization of enterprises, the government proceeded to collectivize agriculture. To this end, it tolerated and even encouraged land seizures. The result was a dramatic drop in food production, with wheat crops declining by almost 50 percent. Acute shortages followed: when Allende's government fell, the country had flour reserves for only a few days.

Protests mounted. The most serious of these were organized by truckers – small private entrepreneurs – who objected to government plans to compete with them by means of a national transport company. On two occasions these strikes, which involved as many as 700,000 people, brought the country's transport and much of the economy to a standstill. In an orthodox Communist country, such demonstrations would have been declared counterrevolutionary plots instigated by the CIA and suppressed. But in Allende's Chile, although the government controlled the radio and much of the press, there remained considerable freedom of information, which could not be silenced without provoking a national revolt. Opposition parties functioned and criticized the government. And, above all, there was the Congress and the Supreme Court.

In August 1973 the Chamber of Deputies voted 81 to 45 that Allende had violated the constitution by usurping its legislative powers, ignoring the country's laws, and infringing on the freedom of speech. The Supreme Court, for its part, condemned Allende for subordinating the judiciary to his political needs. In view of the absence in the Chilean constitution of provisions for impeachment, the Chamber requested the armed forces to restore the laws of the land. Obeying this mandate, eighteen days later, Chile's military, led by General Augusto Pinochet, forcibly removed Allende from office. The new regime was a dictatorship that dealt quite brutally with the defeated socialists and Communists.

Cuba – the first and only enduring Communist state in Latin America – presents an interesting case of a personal dictatorship by an exceedingly ambitious politician who found in

Communist ideology justification for his ambition. In the words of one scholar, 'Historically...Castroism is a leader in search of a movement, a movement in search of power, and power in search of an ideology.'[15]

Contrary to widespread opinion, pre-Communist Cuba was neither a backward nor a predominantly rural country. It had the second-highest living standard in Latin America (after Venezuela, which derived its wealth from petroleum); the majority of its inhabitants were literate and resided in the cities.* Nor is it correct to say that its economy depended on sugar: sugar was indeed the leading export commodity, but it accounted for only one-third or less of national income. In other words, the archetypal preconditions widely believed to account for Communist revolutions – poverty and backwardness – were absent.

The Communists took over Cuba on the wave of essentially middle-class rebellion against the dictatorship of Fulgencio Batista, who in 1952 abolished the democratic constitution that he himself had promulgated during his earlier legitimate terms of office (1933–44). Fidel Castro, the son of a wealthy plantation owner and a student at the Havana Law School, rode to power on this wave of discontent. Although displaying left-wing sympathies he was, to begin with, no Communist:

---

* The experiences of Chile and Cuba may appear to contradict the generalization made at the beginning of this chapter that Communism has the greatest chances of success in countries that have had no experience with democracy and private property. But in neither country did the Communists come to power through social revolution. In Chile, they formed a government peacefully, by agreement with the Christian Democrat Party, which they immediately proceeded to violate. And in Cuba, as will be described below, they took power by leading a national revolt against a despised dictator in the name of restoring democracy.

indeed, he had no ideology at all but only a craving for power. Marxism-Leninism was imbued in him by the Argentinean revolutionary Che Guevara. Castro's program, designed to rally all the classes of the nation behind him, stressed above all the need to restore the 1940 constitution.

Very quickly, however, after assuming dictatorial authority in what was a genuine popular revolution, Castro veered leftward. He introduced a one-party government, carried out a radical land reform, and in 1960, with Soviet encouragement, expropriated all U.S. holdings, which led President Eisenhower to retaliate with a trade embargo. The embargo in turn made Cuba increasingly dependent on the Soviet Union. Moscow, though initially cautious in supporting Castro for fear of U.S. reaction, nevertheless found itself gradually drawn into Cuban politics, especially after April 1961, when Castro proclaimed Cuba a 'socialist' country. The fiasco of the U.S.-instigated Bay of Pigs invasion (April 1961) and the subsequent Cuban Missile Crisis (October 1962), which ended with Washington's pledge to respect Cuban sovereignty, placed the island firmly in the Soviet bloc. During this crisis, Castro had urged Moscow to launch a preemptive nuclear strike against the United States, being prepared to sacrifice Cuba in order to assure the worldwide triumph of 'socialism.'[16] Moscow, which had restrained him, became now the primary economic supporter of Cuba, purchasing a large share of Cuban sugar at artificially high prices, supplying her with oil and many industrial goods, and providing her with generous loans. According to Fidel Castro's brother Raul, before its dissolution the Soviet Union had provided Cuba, free of charge, with $10 billion worth of military equipment. Cuba's economic dependence on Moscow was near total.

In return, Castro loyally supported every Soviet foreign venture, from the invasion of Czechoslovakia to that of Afghanistan; provided Moscow with intelligence listening posts; and undertook to spread Communism throughout Central and Latin America. At its founding congress in Havana in mid-1967, the Castroite Latin American Organization of Solidarity (OLAS) called for guerrilla wars throughout Latin America.

Internally, Castro introduced the standard Soviet-style regime. Within ten years of his ascent to power all sectors of the economy were nationalized, except for agriculture, 30 percent of which was left in the hands of small and medium-sized farmers. The party monopolized politics. Workers, forced to join state-controlled unions, lost the right to organize on their own, to bargain, or to strike. Considerable advances were made in social services – schooling, medicine, housing – financed largely with assets acquired from the pre-Communist economy. Dissent was disposed of in two ways: by allowing a large part of the middle class to emigrate and by creating Soviet-style Revolutionary Tribunals and 'labor camps.'

While it was common for Communist leaders to be deified, most of them preferred to stay in the background, as befitted deities. Not so Castro: he was everywhere, haranguing his captive audiences for hours on end with speeches in which he cajoled, inspired, and threatened. Much of his rhetoric was focused on the United States, which he demonized and blamed for whatever went wrong in Cuba.

Living standards declined relentlessly, in part because of the resistance, mostly passive, of workers and farmers, in part because the most enterprising and best educated Cubans had emigrated to the United States. The survival of the Communist regime came to depend on Soviet support.

Given this reality, the collapse of the Soviet Union and the refusal of the successor Yeltsin government to provide further aid to Cuba seemed to doom the Castro regime. Nevertheless, it managed to survive. It did so by making concessions to foreign capitalists, who were allowed limited but not insignificant opportunities to invest in Cuba. Dollars began to circulate freely in the country. The regime made a major and successful effort to promote tourism, extolling not only Cuba's beaches and cheap resorts but also the beauty and availability of its young women. In 1992, in a speech to the National Assembly, Castro touted the advantages of Cuban prostitution by declaring his country to have the lowest incidence of AIDS. The campaign, which in 1999 brought in 1.7 million foreign tourists, made Cuba 'one of the most popular stops on the sex-vacation circuit, right up there with Thailand.'[17]

If in the case of Mao and even Pol Pot one can still discern, at least in the early phases of their political careers, socialist ideals, in many other regions of the Third World, especially Africa, such a commitment was strikingly absent. Here Marx and Lenin were invoked by ambitious politicians with minimal knowledge of Communist doctrine and history for two purposes: to seize private wealth and to qualify for Communist bloc assistance against domestic and foreign enemies.

A classic example of such fraudulent invocation of Marxism is furnished by the Ethiopian dictator Mengistu Haile Mariam, who between 1974 and 1991 transformed his country into a full-fledged Soviet satellite. Member of a group of army officers disgruntled by slow promotions, Major Mengistu took part in a revolt that in September 1974 overthrew Ethiopia's venerable emperor Haile Selassie. Power passed into the hands of a committee called the Derg, in which Mengistu played a prominent role. Rivalries soon broke up the Derg, and three months later Mengistu staged a military coup in which he took power. He declared Ethiopia a socialist country, a pledge he promptly implemented by nationalizing banks and insurance companies. In March 1975, he abolished private land ownership and forced peasants into communes modeled on Mao's.

In 1976, Mengistu launched his own 'Red Terror': its main victims, numbered in the thousands, were Marxist students. The massacres were carried out with the assistance of some ten thousand security agents supplied by the Soviet Union and East Germany. The Soviet Union, which had initially gained a foothold in the Horn of Africa by backing the 'scientific socialism' proclaimed by a military junta in neighboring Somalia, now abandoned Somalia in favor of Ethiopia. When, in 1977, Somalia invaded Ethiopia with the view of annexing the Ogaden region, the Communist bloc provided Mengistu with massive help, which included a force of up to fifteen thousand Cuban mercenaries. As a result of this military assistance, the Communist bloc gained much influence in Ethiopia. It proved decisive in crushing Somali incursions, as well as the Eritrean movement for independence.

The ruin of the economy, however, brought about by forced collectivization, which was further aggravated by droughts, resulted in famine (1984–85) in which nearly 1 million Ethiopians perished. Following the collapse of East Germany in

1989, Mengistu's internal position deteriorated; by 1991, when the USSR dissolved, the Ethiopian ruler found himself isolated. Overthrown that year, he found refuge in Zimbabwe. Thus ended what has been described as the 'most far-reaching Marxist-Leninist experiment in Africa.'[18]

It is difficult, however, to perceive in nominally 'socialist' Ethiopia anything but a ruthless military dictatorship that aped Soviet and Chinese practices for its own political ends.

As had happened in Western Europe and Japan, in the 1970s and 1980s the Third World witnessed the emergence of terrorist movements that assailed democratic and capitalist institutions in the name of Marxism-Leninism, Stalinism, or Maoism, although they had, in fact, more in common with anarchism.

Typical of the genre was the Communist Party of Peru, popularly known as the 'Shining Path.' Founded by a former professor of philosophy, Abimael Guzmán Reynoso, and composed of young intellectuals, it exploited the grievances of the Indian people to pursue, by means of terror, a Maoist program. Its terrorism claimed twenty-five thousand victims and greatly harmed the Peruvian economy. When Guzmán was captured and put behind bars in 1992, the movement collapsed.

In some other Latin American countries, such as Colombia, 'Marxism' served and continues to serve to give the patina of respectability to armed gangs (the so-called Revolutionary Armed Forces of Colombia and the Army of National Liberation) that combine terror, kidnappings, and extortion with drug trafficking. Since 1964, these two groups have inflicted on Colombia an estimated 120,000 casualties and displaced 2 million people.

Countries living under Communism share striking similarities not only in the means used to bring it into being but also in its consequences. All experience a sharp decline in living standards, often accompanied by famine: droughts seem to have an uncanny affinity for Communist regimes. The loss of civil rights and freedoms rationalized by the need for equality is offset by the emergence of a supreme leader – a generalissimo or *lider máximo* – who concentrates in his hands all the power of which his citizens have been deprived and is elevated to the status of an Oriental divinity. Needless to say, such an outcome is the very antithesis of the Marxist vision, which saw Communism as driven by impersonal economic forces and leading to boundless freedom for all.

VI *Looking Back*

Marxism has been the greatest fantasy of [the twentieth] century.[1]

We are now in a position to address the question posed in the Preface: whether the failure of Communism 'was due to human error or to flaws inherent in its very nature.' The record of history strongly suggests the latter to be the case. Communism was not a good idea that went wrong; it was a bad idea.

From the day the Bolsheviks seized power in Russia in 1917, there have been dozens of attempts made in every part of the world to install societies based on Communist principles. Moscow generously supported them with money, weapons, and guidance. Virtually all failed. In the end, Communism collapsed in Russia, too, and today survives in only a few countries – China, North Korea, Vietnam, and Cuba – and even there it is in the process of erosion: the Communists hold on to power but at the price of making far-reaching concessions to capitalism. Given this dismal record, it is reasonable to assume that there is something flawed either with the premises of Communism or its program or both.

To begin with the dissolution of the Soviet Union, the first Communist country and the motor force that drove

Communist movements globally. Studies published since 1991 have adduced a variety of explanations of this dramatic event: the stagnation of the economy, increased access of Soviet citizens to foreign sources of information, the defeat in Afghanistan, the inability to keep up with the arms race, and so forth. Domestic dissidence, which it was unable to stamp out, and the example of Poland's Solidarity movement unnerved the Soviet leadership. President Reagan's bold challenge to Communism further demoralized the Soviet government, which had come to believe that after the Vietnam debacle the United States had lost the appetite to pursue the Cold War and was ready to withdraw into isolation. Without a doubt, each of these factors played its part. But they would not have brought down a mighty empire had it been a healthy organism. They worked because the organism was sick.

Marxism, the theoretical foundation of Communism, carried within it the seeds of its own destruction, such as Marx and Engels had wrongly attributed to capitalism. It rested on a faulty philosophy of history as well as an unrealistic psychological doctrine.

Marxism's basic contention that private property, which it strives to abolish, is a transient historical phenomenon – an interlude between primitive and advanced Communism – is plainly false. All evidence indicates that land, the main source of wealth in premodern times, unless monopolized by monarchs, had always belonged to tribes, families, or individuals. Livestock as well as commerce and the capital to which it gives rise were always and everywhere in private hands. From which it follows that private property is not a transient phenomenon but a permanent feature of social life and, as such, indestructible.

No less flawed is Marxism's notion that human nature is infinitely malleable, and hence that a combination of coercion and education can produce beings purged of acquisitiveness and willing to dissolve in society at large, a society where, as envisioned by Plato, 'the private and individual is altogether banished from life.' Even if the immense pressures exerted by Communist regimes to this end were to succeed, their success would at best be ephemeral: as animal trainers have discovered, after being subjected to intensive drilling to perform tricks, animals, freed from training, after a while forget what they have learned and revert to their instinctive behavior. Furthermore, given that acquired characteristics are not heritable, each new generation will bring into the world non-Communist attitudes, among which acquisitiveness is certainly not the least powerful. Communism ultimately was defeated by its inability to refashion human nature. Mussolini, who even after turning Fascist viewed Communism with some sympathy, concluded as much in 1920:

> Lenin is an artist who worked on humans as other artists work on marble or metal. But human beings are harder than granite and less malleable than iron. No masterwork has emerged. The artist has failed. The task has proven beyond his powers.[2]

Such realities have forced Communist regimes to resort to violence as a routine means of governance. To compel people to give up what they own and to surrender their private interests to the state requires that public authority dispose of boundless authority. This is what Lenin meant when he defined the 'dictatorship of the proletariat' as 'power that is limited by nothing, by no laws, that is restrained by absolutely no rules, that rests directly on coercion.'

Experience indicates that such a regime is, indeed, feasible: it has been imposed on Russia and its dependencies, on China, Cuba, Vietnam, and Cambodia, as well as on a variety of countries in Africa and Latin America. But its price is not only enormous human suffering; it is also the destruction of the very objective for which such regimes are established, namely equality.

In advocating a regime resting on coercion, Lenin assumed that it would be temporary; its mission accomplished, the coercive state would wither away. He ignored, however, that the abstraction called 'state' is made up of individuals who, whatever their historical mission, attend also to their private interests. Although in Marxist sociology the state serves only the owners of property and has no stake of its own, in reality its stewards quickly evolve into a new class. The 'vanguard party' meant to usher in the new era becomes an end in itself.

The state – or, more precisely, the Communist Party – has no choice but to accommodate this new class because it depends on it to stay in power. And under Communism, the officialdom grows by leaps and bounds for the simple reason that inasmuch as all aspects of national life, the economy very much included, are taken over by the state, it requires a large bureaucracy to administer it. This bureaucracy is the favorite scapegoat of every Communist regime, yet none can manage without it. In the Soviet Union, within a few years of the Bolshevik coup d'état, the regime began to offer unique rewards to its leading cadres, which in time evolved into the *nomenklatura*, a hereditary privileged caste. This spelled the end of the ideal of equality. Thus to enforce the equality of possessions it is necessary to institutionalize inequality of rights.

The contradiction between ends and means is built into Communism and into every country where the state owns all the productive wealth.

True, periodic attempts have been made to shake off the grip that the Communist officialdom secured on the state and society. Lenin and Stalin tried purges, which under Stalin led to mass murder. Mao launched his 'Cultural Revolution' to destroy entrenched party interests. None of these attempts succeeded. In the end, the *nomenklatura*s won out because without them nothing would work.

Attempts to introduce Communism by democratic means also failed. As the experience of Allende's Chile demonstrates, the assault on private property in the presence of a relatively free press, an independent judiciary, and an elected legislature cannot succeed because the opposition, which under a 'dictatorship of the proletariat' is ruthlessly crushed, here has the opportunity to organize resistance. As its numbers swelled, it easily toppled the revolutionary regime. In Nicaragua, where in 1990 the Communist Sandinistas felt enough confidence in their popularity to submit themselves to a popular vote, the people swept them out of power.

The bureaucratization inherent in Communist regimes was also responsible for the economic failures that either contributed to their downfall or else compelled them to abandon Communism in all but name. The nationalization of productive assets led to the transfer of their management to officials who had neither the competence nor the motivation to operate them efficiently. The inevitable result was declining productivity. Furthermore, the rigidity inherent in centralized management made Communist economies unresponsive to technological innovation, which explains why the Soviet Union, despite its high level of science, missed out on some of the most important technological discoveries of recent times. As Friedrich Hayek has pointed out, only the free market has the ability to sense and respond to shifts in the economy. And only the prospect of enrichment motivates people to exert themselves beyond their immediate needs. Under Communism, effective incentives were lacking: indeed, diligence at work was punished, in that meeting one's productivity quotas resulted in these quotas being raised.

The failures of Communist economic policy had the most tragic consequences in agriculture, the basis of the economy of nearly all countries subjected to Communist rule. The confiscation of private property in land and the collectivization that ensued disrupted traditional rural routines, causing famines of unprecedented dimensions. This happened in the Soviet Union, China, Cambodia, Ethiopia, and North Korea; in each country millions died from man-made starvation. In Communist North Korea as late as the 1990s, a large proportion of children suffered from physical disabilities caused by malnutrition; in the second half of the 1990s, up to 2 million people are estimated to have died of starvation there. Its infant mortality rate is 88 per 1,000 live births, compared to South Korea's 8, and the life expectancy for males 48.9 years, compared to South Korea's 70.4. The GDP per capita in the north is $900; in the south, $13,700.

Nor are the inability to provide abundance and enforce equality, its alleged objectives, the only contradictions inherent in Communism. Another is the lack of freedom which, along with prosperity and equality, was for Marx an ultimate goal of his movement. The nationalization of all productive resources turns all citizens into state employees – in other words, dependents of the government. In the words of Trotsky's 'Revolution Betrayed': 'In a country where the sole employer is the state, opposition means slow starvation. The old principle, who does not work shall not eat, has been replaced by a new one: who does not obey shall not eat.' Only the recognition by the state of the rights of its subjects and citizens to their belongings – and respect shown to that right – imposes limits on state power. And inasmuch as property is a legal concept, enforced by courts, it also signifies acknowledgment that the state is bound by law. This means that the goal of Communism, the abolition of property, inevitably leads to the abolition of liberty and legality. The nationalization of productive resources, far from liberating men from enslavement by things, as Marx and Engels had envisioned, converts them into slaves of their rulers and, because of endemic shortages, makes them more materialistic than ever.

So much for attempts to introduce Communism within national boundaries. Matters did not look much better for Communism on the international scale. Because they viewed capitalism as global, Marxists insisted that its abolition had to be global as well: the slogan 'Proletarians of all countries, unite!,' launched by the *Communist Manifesto* of 1848 and subsequently adopted by socialists as well as Communists, posited the solidarity of labor across boundaries.

Such unity proved fictitious. Whatever affinities people may feel toward their class, territorial and ethnic loyalties always and everywhere evoke stronger emotions. Whenever they are challenged by foreign powers, classes close ranks. The socialists learned this lesson in 1914 when, contrary to repeated pledges, the national parties of the Second International almost without exception backed their 'bourgeois' governments and voted for war. Lenin relearned it in 1920 when Polish workers and peasants rallied to defend their country from the invading Red Army come to 'liberate' them from exploitation. This experience recurred time and again.

Nor was it confined to so-called class societies. Even countries ruled by Communist governments, formally classless, chafed under Soviet domination and, whenever given a chance, broke loose of it. This happened first in Yugoslavia but most strikingly in China. Within a decade of coming to power, the Chinese Communists claimed the right to practice and spread their own brand of Marxism and, to assert it, nearly waged war against the Soviet Union, their model and mentor. The Khmer Rouge went even further, seeking total self-sufficiency and insisting that its kind of Communism had nothing in common with the Russian or the Chinese. European Communist movements similarly demanded pluralism ('polycentrism') even when Soviet power was at its height.

The only way Moscow could neutralize these centrifugal forces within the international movement was by keeping the foreign Communist parties weak and hence fully dependent on it; for as soon as their constituencies expanded, these parties demanded autonomy and even independence. Hence the dilemma: the international Communist movement either remained isolated and impotent, an obedient tool of Moscow but of limited utility to it, or else it grew strong and influential, in which case it emancipated itself from Moscow, wrecking the unity of international Communism. There was no third alternative.

These inherent flaws were acknowledged by many Communists, leading to various 'revisionisms.' To the true believers, however, the failures proved not that the doctrine was wrong but that it had not been applied with sufficient ruthlessness. Confirming Santayana's definition of fanatics as people who redouble their efforts after forgetting their aim, they went on killing sprees of mounting savagery. Thus Communism generated ever greater oceans of blood as it progressed from Lenin to Stalin, and from Stalin to Mao and Pol Pot.

In sum, Communism failed and is bound to fail for at least two reasons: one, that to enforce equality, its principal objective, it is necessary to create a coercive apparatus that demands privileges and thereby negates equality; and two, that ethnic and territorial loyalties, when in conflict with class allegiances, everywhere and at all times overwhelm them, dissolving Communism in nationalism, which is why socialism so easily combines with 'Fascism.' In recognition of this reality, the Communist Party of the Russian Federation, the post-1990 successor to the Communist Party of the Soviet Union, abandoned the slogan calling on proletarians of all countries to unite.

Anticipating these developments, the German-Italian sociologist Robert Michels correctly predicted that 'socialists may triumph but socialism never.'

There is also a further, more specific reason connected with the structure of Communist regimes as devised by Lenin that militates against the realization of the Communist ideal. Assuming that the global collapse of capitalism was imminent, Lenin organized his government on a military model: Soviet

Communism and its emulators militarized politics, subordinating it to a central command. This structure, by virtue of its ability to mobilize all human and natural resources, proved effective in fending off direct physical challenges to the regime and expanding its influence abroad. It turned out to be far less effective – indeed, impotent – in coping with challenges that could not be resolved by force. When the expected world revolution did not occur, the Soviet regime ossified, as it were, and in time found itself threatened by internal difficulties, such as apathy and passivity of the population, which led to a steady decline of the economy and the military power resting on it. These could be resolved only by the regime relaxing its authority.

But relaxation of authority subverted the whole Communist regime, which was of a piece and depended on a strictly centralized command organization. As soon as Gorbachev began to tamper with the system, it developed fissures and before long flew apart. In this sense, Communism was unreformable, which is to say, incapable of adjusting to changing circumstances. Its inherent rigidity led to its downfall.

One of the controversial subjects in the history of Communism is the role played in it by ideology – specifically that labeled Marxism-Leninism. Some scholars believe that the movement and the regime to which it gave rise were driven by ideas, for which reason they refer to the Soviet Union and Maoist China as 'ideocracies,' that is, systems ruled by ideas.

It is, of course, true that Communism would not have come into being were it not for the myth of the Golden Age and the doctrine conceived by Marx and first implemented by Lenin, which provided a strategy for how to bring it back. But to concede this is not tantamount to accepting the notion of 'ideocracy,' simply because all ideas, political and economic alike, once they are implemented, give rise to power and soon turn into its tools. The capitalist economy found its classic formulation in Adam Smith's *Wealth of Nations*. Yet no one would seriously maintain that capitalists of the past two centuries have acted as they did under the influence of Smith's idea of the 'invisible hand' or any other element of his theory. The thrust of his ideas served the capitalists' interests, and for this reason they adopted them.

There are no grounds for believing that the same does not hold true of Marxism-Leninism. The notion that millions of Communist Party members and state functionaries were committed to theories conceived by a nineteenth-century German economist is surely a conceit entertained by intellectuals, some of whom seem to believe that humanity is driven by ideas. When they first come into being, Communist parties are usually small and often persecuted; membership in them carries more risks than benefits, for which reason a high proportion of their members may well be ideologically motivated. But once they are in power, dispensing privileges as well as punishments, such parties attract a mass following, which pays merely lip service to the reigning ideology. A 1922 survey of Communist Party members in the Soviet Union revealed that only 0.6 percent had completed higher education and only 6.4 percent had secondary-school diplomas. On the basis of such evidence, one Russian historian concluded that 92.7 percent of the party's membership was functionally illiterate (4.7 percent was literally illiterate), facts of which Lenin was painfully aware when in 1921 he ordered the first 'purge' of party cadres to rid it of 'opportunists.' It was a futile effort to stem the inevitable. As the Communist state assumes ever greater responsibilities, its ranks expand relentlessly by the influx of careerists, for whom party membership signifies security and entitlements. Power becomes an end in itself, and so does self-preservation. Ideas by then become little more than fig leaves with which to hide the true nature of the regime, flaunting high-sounding ideals while pursuing the most mundane objectives and engaging in the most odious behavior.

It is significant that when the Soviet government disintegrated in 1991, the supposed guardians of ideological purity – the *nomenklatura* – gave up without a fight and pounced on the country's natural resources and manufactures, stripping them bare, under the guise of 'privatization,' for their personal benefit. This would scarcely have happened if the apparatus had indeed been committed to Marxist-Leninist ideology.

Interesting evidence of the secondary role that Marxist ideology has played in Communist politics is provided by the biography of Nikita Khrushchev, Stalin's successor and the ruler of the Soviet Union from 1953 to 1964, written by his son, Sergei. 'Ever since my student days,' the young Khrushchev writes,

> I had tried and failed to understand what exactly communism was....I had tried to get Father to shed light on the nature of communism, but did not get any intelligible answer then either. I understood that he was not very clear about it himself.[3]

And if the leader of the Communist bloc and the tireless herald of its coming worldwide triumph could not explain to his son what Communism was, what can one expect of the theoretical understanding of the rank and file?

It is self-interest – personal as well as national – that propelled Communist regimes and undercut its egalitarian ideals. How often and how unceremoniously Soviet leaders and Chinese leaders departed from the Marxist canon when it suited their interests! In 1917, Lenin allowed workers to take over factories and peasants to seize land, although these anarchist actions violated Marxist doctrine. In 1921, he restored the free market in agricultural produce and allowed capitalist enterprise in consumer goods. Stalin gave collective farmers private plots, the produce of which they could sell at negotiated prices. In the 1930s he encouraged abroad Popular Fronts, which entailed collaboration between Communists and their archenemies, the Social Democrats. Khrushchev replaced international class war with 'peaceful coexistence.' Mao pronounced the human will capable of triumphing over objective reality, while his successors have been encouraging their subjects to enrich themselves. All this was done in the name of Communism. In each case, the requirements of ideology were sacrificed, at any rate temporarily, to the supreme needs of the party, which were always and everywhere the same: the maintenance and expansion of unlimited power.

The costs of the experiments in utopia were staggering. They took a huge toll on human lives. Stéphane Courtois, the editor of *The Black Book of Communism*, estimates the global number of Communism's victims at between 85 and 100 million, which is 50 percent greater than the deaths caused by the two world wars. Various justifications have been offered for these losses, such as that one cannot make an omelette without breaking eggs. Apart from the fact that human beings are not eggs, the trouble is that no omelette has emerged from the slaughter.

The survivors, too, paid a price. In their effort to impose total conformity, Communist regimes drove into exile, incarcerated, and silenced those who would not conform – often the ablest and most enterprising. As a result something like reverse evolution was set in motion, with the most dependent and conformist having the best chance of survival. The enterprising, truthful, and public-minded perished. Communist societies thus lost the best and found themselves correspondingly impoverished.

In Russia, which experienced Communism the longest, one of the effects is that the population has been robbed of self-reliance. Since under the Soviet regime all orders pertaining to nonpersonal affairs had to emanate from above and initiative was treated as a crime, the nation has lost the ability to make decisions, whether in big or small matters (except where criminal enterprise is concerned); people wait for orders. After a brief outburst of enthusiasm for democracy, the yearning for a strong guiding hand reasserted itself. The nation has found itself both incapable and unwilling to stand on its own feet and take charge of its destiny. This is not the least of the harm that Communism has inflicted on Russia and all countries that, like it, have been subjected to prolonged Communist dressage. It has also killed in them the work ethic and a sense of public responsibility.

Acquisitiveness is inborn; respect for the acquisitions of others is learned. This much is known from child psychology.

From which it follows that if an individual finds that others – be it government or society at large – do not respect his property rights he not only loses regard for their belongings but develops the most rapacious instincts. This is precisely what happened after the collapse of the Communist regime in the USSR, hampering the transition to a genuine market economy, which rests on respect for property rights.

Marx maintained that capitalism suffered from insoluble internal contradictions, which doomed it to destruction. In reality, capitalism, being an empirical system responsive to realities and capable of adjustments, has managed to overcome every one of its crises. Communism, on the other hand, being a rigid doctrine – a pseudoscience converted into a pseudo-religion and embodied in an inflexible political regime – has proven incapable of shedding the misconceptions to which it was beholden and gave up the ghost. If it is ever revived, it will be in defiance of history and with the certainty of yet another costly failure. Such action will border on madness, which has been defined as doing the same thing over and over and expecting different results.

Notes

1 Kitty Muggeridge and Ruth Adam, *Beatrice Webb* (New York, 1968), 243, written in 1934 or 1935.

I Communist Theory and Program

1 *Capital*, vol. I, chapter xxxii.
2 K. Marx and F. Engels, *Collected Works*, vol. III (New York, 1975), 393.
3 George Lukacs, *History and Class Consciousness* (Cambridge, Mass., 1971), 315.
4 *German Ideology*, in Marx and Engels, *Collected Works*, vol. V (New York, 1976), 47.

II Leninism

1 Naum Jasny, *The Socialized Agriculture of the USSR* (Stanford, 1949), 145–46.
2 Richard Pipes, *A Concise History of the Russian Revolution* (New York, 1995), 121n.
3 V. I. Lenin, *Polnoe sobranie sochinenii*, 5th ed. (Moscow, 1958–65), vol. 41, 383.
4 Richard Pipes, *The Russian Revolution* (New York, 1990), 696.
5 L. N. Kritsman, *Geroicheskii period velikoi russkoi revoliutsii* (Moscow, 1926), 166.
6 Isaac Steinberg, *In the Workshop of the Revolution* (London, 1955), 145.
7 Lenin, *Polnoe sobranie sochinenii*, vol. 37, 39–41.
8 Richard Pipes, ed., *The Unknown Lenin* (New Haven, Conn., 1996), 50.

9 A. G. Latyshev, *Rassekrechennyi Lenin* (Moscow, 1996), 40. This passage was omitted from Lenin's *Polnoe sobranie sochinenii* (Complete Works), 5th ed.

10 Lenin, *Polnoe sobranie sochinenii*, vol. 42, 1.

11 Clara Zetkin, *Reminiscences of Lenin* (London, 1929), 20.

III Stalin and After

1 Pipes, *Unknown Lenin*, 152–53.

2 Mikhail Heller and Aleksandr Nekrich, *Utopia in Power: The History of the Soviet Union from 1917 to the Present* (New York, 1986), 201.

3 Alec Nove, *An Economic History of the USSR* (London, 1988), 208.

4 Nicholas Werth in Stéphane Courtois, ed., *The Black Book of Communism* (Cambridge, Mass., 1999), 153, 155.

5 *Ibid.*, 162.

6 Nove, *Economic History*, 243.

7 Werth in Courtois, *The Black Book of Communism*, 159, 167.

8 M. B. Olcott in *Russian Review*, vol. XL, no. 2 (1981), 122, 136.

9 *Hoy* (Havana), February 24, 1963, cited in Theodore Draper, *Castroism: Theory and Practice* (New York, 1965), 217–18.

10 Alfred Mirek, *Krasnyi mirazh* (Moscow, 2000), 265–66.

11 Vladimir Naumov in William Taubman et al., eds., *Nikita Khrushchev* (New Haven, Conn., 2000), 90.

12 Sheila Fitzpatrick, *Everyday Stalinism* (New York, 1999), 127.

13 Bertram D. Wolfe, ed., *Khrushchev and Stalin's Ghost* (New York, 1957), 124.

14 David Remnick, *Lenin's Tomb* (New York, 1993), 406.

15 Michael Voslensky, *Nomenklatura: The Soviet Ruling Class* (Garden City, N.Y., 1984), 61.

16 Remnick, *Lenin's Tomb*, 172–73.

17 *The New York Times*, August 15, 2000, p. A7.

18 R. G. Pikhoia, *Sovetskii Soiuz: Istoriia vlasti, 1945–1991* (Moscow, 1998), 140.

19 *Sistema ispravitel' no-trudovykh lagerei v SSSR, 1923–1960* (Moscow, 1998), 48.

20 Nove, *Economic History*, 180.
21 Karl Marx, *The Class Struggles in France* (New York, 1964), 114. Emphasis added.
22 Louis Fischer in Richard Crossman, ed., *The God That Failed* (New York, 1949), 205.
23 Nadezhda Mandelstam, *Hope Against Hope* (New York, 1970), 13. Translation by Max Hayward.
24 M. Gorki, *Lenine et le Paysan Russe* (Paris, 1924), 64.
25 Henry Picker, ed., *Hitlers Tischgespräche im Führerhauptquartier, 1941–1942* (Bonn, 1951), 133.
26 *Sto sorok besed s Molotovym: Iz dnevnika F. Chueva* (Moscow, 1991), 184.
27 I. V. Stalin, *Sochineniia*, vol. 7 (Moscow, 1952), 27, 14. Emphasis added.
28 John Erickson and David Dilks, eds., *Barbarossa: The Axis and the Allies* (Edinburgh, 1994), 261.
29 Leonard Schapiro in George Urban, ed., *Stalinism* (New York, 1982), 423.
30 Andrej Sinjawskij, *Der Traum vom neuen Menschen oder die So-wjetzivilisation* (Frankfurt, 1989), 262–63.
31 Robert W. Pringle in *International Journal of Intelligence and Counterintelligence*, Summer 2000, 195.
32 Markus Wolf, *The Man Without a Face* (London, 1997), 218–19.

IV Reception in the West

1 Jane Degras, ed., *The Communist International, 1919–1943: Documents*, vol. I (London, 1956), 128.
2 Pipes, ed., *The Unknown Lenin*, 90.
3 Lenin, *Polnoe sobranie sochinenii*, vol. 41, 38.
4 Degras, *The Communist International*, vol. I, 166–72.
5 Arthur Koestler, *The Invisible Writing* (New York, 1954), 53.
6 In Crossman, ed., *The God That Failed*, 23.
7 *The Times* (London), February 11, 1920, p. 9.
8 Lenin, *Polnoe sobranie sochinenii*, vol. 49, 15, and vol. 38, 139.
9 Carl J. Friedrich, *Totalitarianism* (Cambridge, Mass., 1954), 49.
10 Hans Buchheim, *Totalitarian Rule* (Middletown, Conn., 1968), 38–39.

11 Benito Mussolini, *Opera omnia*, vol. XVII (Florence, 1955), 295.

12 Picker, ed., *Hitlers Tischgespräche*, 133.

13 *The New York Times*, August 11, 1990, p. A2.

14 *Ibid.*, June 18, 1992, p. A18.

15 David Childs, ed., *The Changing Face of Western Communism* (London, 1980), 276.

v The Third World

1 Courtois in *The Black Book of Communism*, 754.

2 François Ponchaud in Karl D. Jackson, ed., *Cambodia 1975–1978: Rendezvous with Death* (Princeton, 1989), 152.

3 Pipes, ed., *The Unknown Lenin*, 121.

4 Leszek Kolakowski, *Main Currents of Marxism*, vol. III (Oxford, 1978), 495, 521.

5 Marx and Engels, 'The German Ideology,' in *Collected Works*, vol. V, 37.

6 *Quotations from Chairman Mao Tse-tung* (New York, 1968), 32–33.

7 *Ibid.*, 77.

8 Stuart Schram, *Mao Tse-tung* (Harmondsworth, U.K., 1966), 291.

9 Donald S. Zagoria, *The Sino-Soviet Conflict, 1956–1961* (New York, 1964), 385.

10 *Quotations from Chairman Mao Tse-tung*, 19–20.

11 Jasper Becker, *Hungry Ghosts: China's Secret Famine* (London, 1996), p. xi.

12 Kenneth M. Quinn in Jackson, *Cambodia*, 238.

13 Jackson, *Cambodia*, 3 and 150.

14 Charles M. Twining in Jackson, *Cambodia*, 110.

15 Draper, *Castroism*, 48–49.

16 Sergei Khrushchev, *Nikita Khrushchev* (University Park, Pa., 2000), 627.

17 Silvana Paternostro in *The New Republic*, July 10–17, 2000, 20.

18 Peter Woodward, *The Horn of Africa* (London and New York, 1996), 99.

VI Looking Back

1 Kolakowski, *Main Currents*, vol. III, 523.
2 Mussolini, *Opera omnia*, vol. XV (Florence, 1954), 93.
3 Sergei Khrushchev, *Nikita Khrushchev*, 701.

Suggestions for Further Reading

The literature on Communist theory and practice is, for all practical purposes, inexhaustible; the library of Harvard University lists over 20,000 volumes devoted exclusively to this subject. General works dealing with it, along with journal and newspaper articles, undoubtedly run into the hundreds of thousands. The Harvard catalog records 3,567 titles for Marx and 4,301 for Lenin. Hence any brief bibliography on the topic of this book must of necessity be very selective and arbitrary. But since most of the books enumerated below have their own lists of suggested readings, the reader interested in pursuing further any topic should have no difficulty securing bibliographic guidance.

The intellectual history of the Golden Age theme is told in Frank E. Manuel and Fritzie P. Manuel, *Utopian Thought in the Western World* (Cambridge, Mass., 1979). Alexander Gray's *The Socialist Tradition: Moses to Lenin* (London, 1963) supplements it. The standard work on Marxism and its various offspring is Leszek Kolakowski's *Main Currents of Marxism*, 3 vols. (Oxford, 1978). Andrzej Walicki's *Marxism and the Leap to the Kingdom of Freedom* (Stanford, 1995) demonstrates the link between Marxist theory and Communist practice. The First and Second Internationals are treated in Julius

Braunthal's *History of the International*, 2 vols. (New York, 1967).

On revolutionary Russia, the reader may wish to consult my *Russian Revolution* (New York, 1990) and *Russia Under the Bolshevik Regime* (New York, 1994). A condensation of the two volumes appeared as *A Concise History of the Russian Revolution* (New York, 1995). A different appraisal of these events can be found in Sheila Fitzpatrick's *The Russian Revolution*, 2nd ed. (Oxford and New York, 1994). Two eminent Russian writers left eyewitness accounts of the revolution: Ivan Bunin, *Cursed Days* (Chicago, 1998), and Maxim Gorky, *Untimely Thoughts* (New Haven, Conn., 1995).

The life of the Soviet Union's founder, using previously secreted archival sources, has been written by Dmitrii Volkogonov, in *Lenin: A New Biography* (New York, 1994). Volkogonov is also the author of *Stalin: Triumph and Tragedy* (New York, 1991). A well-informed account of the Stalin era is Roy Medvedev's *Let History Judge* (New York, 1989).

There is a reliable survey of Soviet history written by two Russian émigrés, Mikhail Heller and Aleksandr Nekrich, *Utopia in Power: The History of the Soviet Union from 1917 to the Present* (New York, 1986). The central institution of the Soviet state is the subject of a monograph by Leonard Schapiro, *The Communist Party of the Soviet Union*, 2nd ed. (London, 1970). Milovan Djilas, a high-level Serbian Communist, in his *The New Class* (New York, 1957) was among the first to alert the world to the existence in the USSR of a new elite, the privileges of which are the subject of Michael Voslensky's

Nomenklatura: The Soviet Ruling Class (Garden City, N.Y., 1984). Alec Nove's *An Economic History of the USSR* (London, 1988) is succinct and authoritative.

Aleksandr Solzhenitsyn has written a documentary history of the Soviet forced labor system: *The Gulag Archipelago*, 3 vols. (New York, 1991–92). The story of Stalin's massacres is recounted in Robert Conquest's *The Great Terror: A Reassessment* (New York, 1990).

The attraction of foreign intellectuals to Communism is told in Paul Hollander's *Political Pilgrims: Travels of Western Intellectuals to the Soviet Union and China and Cuba* (New York, 1981). The disillusionment of six prominent writers among them is the subject of Richard Crossman, ed., *The God That Failed* (New York, 1949).

The foreign policy of the USSR during its first half century is treated by George Kennan in *Russia and the West Under Lenin and Stalin* (Boston, 1961) and by Adam Ulam in *Expansion and Coexistence: The History of Soviet Foreign Policy, 1917–67* (New York, 1968). The Soviet Union's relations with the West from the end of World War II until the Cuban Missile Crisis of 1962 are traced in John Lewis Gaddis's *We Now Know: Rethinking Cold War History* (New York, 1997).

The basic documents of the Comintern have been assembled by Jane Degras in *The Communist International, 1919–1943*, 3 vols. (London, 1956–71). Its history is recounted by Franz Borkenau in *World Communism: A History of the Communist International* (Ann Arbor, 1962) and, more recently, by Kevin McDermott and Jeremy Agnew in *The Comintern* (London, 1996).

The collapse of the Soviet Union is vividly told, using personal observations and conversations, by David Remnick in *Lenin's Tomb* (New York, 1993).

The history of Communist China until 1982 is covered in parts 1 and 2, volumes XIV and XV of Roderick MacFarquhar and John K. Fairbank, eds., *The Cambridge History of China* (1987, 1991). Mao's philosophy of history is best documented in his own *Quotations from Chairman Mao Tse-tung* (New York, 1968). His political and intellectual biography can be found in Stuart Schram's *Mao Tse-tung* (Penguin Books, 1974). His life is told by Ross Terrill in *A Biography of Mao* (Stanford, 1999).

The Pol Pot period in Cambodian history is described in a collective work edited by Karl D. Jackson, *Cambodia 1975–1978: Rendezvous with Death* (Princeton, 1989).

On Castro and Communism in Cuba, I found particularly informative an older work by Theodore Draper, *Castroism: Theory and Practice* (New York, 1965), and a newer one by Susan Eva Eckstein, *Back from the Future: Cuba Under Castro* (Princeton, 1994).

Communism in East Africa is the subject of Peter Woodward's *The Horn of Africa* (London and New York, 1996) and Paul Henze's *Horn of Africa: From War to Peace* (New York, 1991).

On the Chilean Communist episode, the reader may consult Robert J. Alexander's *The Tragedy of Chile* (Westport, Conn., 1978) and Paul E. Sigmund's *The Overthrow of Allende and Politics of Chile, 1964–1976* (Pittsburgh, 1977).

The human cost of twentieth-century Communism globally is depicted and estimated in a book edited by Stéphane Courtois, *The Black Book of Communism* (Cambridge, Mass., 1999).

Index